IMPACT WARFARE

**Engaging End-Times Spiritual Warfare
In Dynamic Prayer & With Maximum Impact**

By

B. James Howells

IMPACT WARFARE: ENGAGING END-TIMES SPIRITUAL WARFARE IN DYNAMIC PRAYER AND WITH MAXIMUM IMPACT
BY: B. James Howells

This book is dedicated to:

The Watchmen on the walls...those standing in the gap...to the prayer warriors...and to all those mighty men and women of God who serve in the name and blood of JESUS CHRIST.

For my Father, for my Savior, for my Comforter...

Table of Contents

Introduction

"They just don't take it seriously at all. I don't have that luxury, it would cost me too much. All that I care about depends on me taking seriously every moment that I serve and fight for what I believe."

Tears well up in my eyes even now as I write those words above. I remember their sting when I first heard them from one of my oldest and dearest friends, who is not a believer, but he hit the nail on the head. His statement stung my heart because I knew he was right and that they were the truth.

I asked my friend what he felt the major difference was between warriors like himself and Christians engaged in spiritual warfare who seem either overtaken by the battles they face or are completely unaware of what is going on around them. His answer has meaning because he is someone

7

who knows what he is talking about as he serves in a U.S. Army special forces unit and lives in active combat as a part of daily life. He lives a life of impact.

For years I have watched my fellow Christians become mired in defeat. I have seen ineffectual ministry leave people weak, wanting, and torn apart by physical and spiritual sickness and disease. I have watched the church accept this as normal while its leaders struggle in places where we have victory, and they are frequently overcome by forces we have power to stand against. I have seen the casualness of a sleeping church that not only takes the spiritual with no seriousness, but which seriously has left its people ill-prepared for the battle in which we live every day.

If you are still reading this, I need you to hear something... the church has fallen asleep when it comes to spiritual warfare!

We have forgotten the power that Jesus left us to operate in. We have relegated spiritual gifts and power to the prophets of old, the 1ˢᵗ century Christians, or worse to the realm of bedtime story and myth. **Because we see no evidence of them in action, we think it evident that they are no longer active** and available to us today, save by some rare miracle or extra-ordinary occurrence. In reality, nothing could be further from the truth.

The words of Jesus that He spoke to His church have never been taken back; "*Heal the sick, cleanse the lepers, raise the dead, cast out devils*" (Matthew 10:8) and "*Behold, I give unto you power to tread on serpents and scorpions, and over all the power of the enemy*" (Luke 10:19). What Christ freely gave to His church is still active in His church today.

Impact

"Impact" is a word that all special operators and warriors know well. It is a defining term for the passion of how they live, how they fight, and how they engage in almost all matters. It is the how and why behind everything of purpose for them.

Merriam-Webster defines the term impact as; "to have a direct effect or impact on, the force of impression of one thing on another: a significant or major effect."

I have lived my life around men and women of impact. It is what has led to the drive in me to approach all challenges, obstacles and opportunities of life with meaning and purpose. It is also why I take so seriously the calling God has placed upon my heart as I have seen how the supernatural knows, lives, and understands impact and affect. I have seen how the darkness embraces these principles to have victory in the battles they engage us in and how the Church has lost this understanding and victory.

My introduction to the impact mindset and way of living came through unique individuals many never have the chance of meeting, let alone to train under or to have open access to, and to opportunities that only God could have orchestrated and kept me through.

I have known and trained with men and women in intelligence, psychological operations, special forces, combat control teams and emergency management. I have studied under and have been mentored by apologists, evangelists, theologians, preachers, rabbis, mystics, "holy men" and prophecy experts. And, I have spent time with and learned amazing things from mathematicians, engineers, DARPA & JASON scientists, politicians and intellectuals. All of whom have expanded my paradigm, challenged my capabilities and broadened my understanding of so many things.

I am not stating any of this to brag or compare notes with anyone. No, I share this because this intensive training, interaction, and experiences became coupled with a life of deep biblical study and decades of research. I have spent over thirty years in scripture and twenty-five years engaged in spiritual warfare with the occult and supernatural. I have learned more than I ever wanted to know about the darkness we face and how we have fallen to its schemes and lies because we have forgotten the impact we are in Christ…an impact of dynamic affect!

Warfare

We have lost the realization and appreciation that what we live and serve in is active and very real warfare and battle. *"For we wrestle not against flesh and blood, but against principalities, against powers, against the rulers of the darkness of this world, against spiritual wickedness in high places"* (Ephesians 6:12).

We battle, as Christians, against entities much more powerful, intelligent, and aggressive than any flesh and blood enemy. We strive to exist in a world ruled by forces intent on our demise, our elimination, and our corruption. Yet even though we are warned of this battle, we appear to not fully grasp that this is war, and we exist in warfare raging all around us physical and spiritual.

We have believers who cannot see the darkness they play with every week in their use of socially acceptable occult practices and we have untrained warriors going into action against the spiritual realm only to become fodder for the forces they do not understand. We are held captive by that which we have been granted the almighty and absolute power to proclaim freedom and deliverance from.

There is good news though...*The* Good News! We do not fight in this warfare alone and the war has already been won, we have victory in Jesus Christ. So, let's stand up and claim the rights He has won for us.

I see the approaching horizon, as do many of you reading this. I see us entering the throws of the end-times and a time of great delusion and strife...and I see men and women of God standing up once more and standing in the promises and power of the Lord our God!

I see spiritual warfare no longer a sideshow, or in the shadows of the church, but becoming a term of strength and a real force in the church again, and deliverance becoming a sought-after ministry once more. The Holy Spirit is beginning to stir up the end-times believers in a way we have not seen for millennia.

The Church is ready to have impact again, to exhibit maximum impact against the darkness which seems to be growing stronger each day, and for the followers of Christ to again be warriors of impact in this ancient and old battle that rages around us.

Impact is not meant to be a term for casual occurrences or brushing contact. No, Impact denotes forceful and event/life changing contact. It is a term suited for warfare....

Warfare is no longer to be a term of anxiety, nor is it to be shied away from in the pulpit any longer. It is time we embrace this term and live in this reality and paradigm. We are victors in Christ, we are children of the living God who is coming soon to claim His prize!

The Path Ahead

This book is not just for the select spiritual warfare and deliverance ministers who we see as standing on the forward edge of the battle... it is for every person who seeks Christ and will begin to come against these forces and for all who call themselves Christian standing and living in battle daily with these higher entities.

I have put this work together into two parts. This is not due to its length, as this is in no way a comprehensive compendium on spiritual warfare, but to make the best impact overall for the reader.

Part one develops an understanding of the Holy Spirit, and what I call an Impact Warrior. It will go over what I have found to be the foundation, the character, as well as the gear and tactics of warfare that this warrior engages in and battles within. We will learn how to serve to our utmost. Part one is going to equip us so that we can operate as the elite spiritual sons and daughters that God has adopted into His family.

Part two is going to take us deep into the most potent of weapons which we must wield effectively and the most essential form of communication we have in this warfare...prayer! We will look at what I call Impact Prayer. This is prayer not just for our asking and praise, it is an atomic weapon that can shake the battlefield and destroy strongholds of the enemy.

Let us encourage each other and come together in spiritual warfare and prayer as the church has done in ages past. Let us take this with the seriousness it demands and with the joy that comes from serving our God. Let us strive to live and serve as Paul when he states, "*I have fought the good fight, I have finished the race, I have kept the faith.*" (2 Timothy 4:7)

IMPACT WARFARE

PART I: Impact Warrior

When you speak about what it takes to stand as a warrior, the very first absolute is always this.... If the individual does not believe that what he stands for, fights for, and is giving his life for is true... if the very fundamental cause which has brought him to the battle is not the burning fire of every heartbeat and breath... then he will not fight long, he will not fight hard, and he will not stay the course.

So, we must start with the truth. Jesus Christ is our Lord and savior, He died for our sin, He rose from the dead, ascended into heaven, and He is coming back soon. This belief is the cause for which we stand, we fight, and we persevere.

If you have not made Jesus Christ your Lord and savior, if you do not know Jesus personally, and He is not the primal cause of your life... then please stop reading any further and seek Him first. Find a bible believing church, find a friend or loved one who knows Christ, or find my contact information and reach out to me personally. Get to know Jesus, hear the Gospel message, start with giving your life to Christ before endeavoring to stand and build your character to be a warrior in these end-times. This is not a game; your eternal life depends on it.

If Jesus Christ is your Lord, if He is the very beat of your heart and the very cause of your life and your stand...then let us journey together into the character of a warrior and the makeup of our combat.

But, before we jump right into the traits and makeup of the Impact Warrior, let's begin by knowing the one inside us that brings forth the character of God and the power in all we do.

The Warrior Spirit

*"Even the Spirit of truth; whom the world cannot receive,
because it seeth him not, neither knoweth him: but ye know
him; for he dwelleth with you, and shall be in you."*
(John 14:16-17).

Pneuma is a Greek word which is used for the Holy Spirit in
scripture and this is the Ruach Ha'Kodesh of the old testament
Hebrew. This name for the Holy Spirit means power manifest
as we shall see.

Lexico.com defines this for us as; "containing or
operated by air or gas under pressure", or even better yet,
**"(chiefly in the context of New Testament theology)
relating to the Spirit."**

Special Forces Operators and Martial Artists use the
word "spirit" often when they speak of that power of will and

individual force that percolates within them. This is a presence within that has been called the "warrior spirit" and it is a powerful part of what pushes and drives an individual to press on amidst struggle, adversity, and against all odds. For the Christian, they know that the spirit and will of man are useless in the battles we fight and live within.

A Will and Spirit Greater than Ours

When we submit to the Will of God and allow the Holy Spirit to be the force behind the tools we have and use in obedience to our calling...something exponentially amazing occurs. With minimal effort on our part, these tools now have maximum effect, and affect the world around us both natural and supernatural. In life we have a very fitting illustration and example of this in action.

Every tradesman has tools they utilize. Some are simple hand tools, others are power tools. They know which tool is right to use and best for the desired result. And when it comes to jobs which require a lot of directed power, jobs which require extreme effort that would tax or burn out the typical tools of the trade, they turn to a specific type of tool...pneumatic tools.

Pneumatic tools (tools operated by pneuma) convert compressed air into force to deliver impact like nothing else, hence why they are often referred to as "impact tools". These tools deliver maximum torque with minimal effort on the part of the user. Their power lies in the "Pneuma" they have coursing through them.

The difference between operating by our spirit and operating in His Spirit…is the same as the difference between simple tools and impact tools.

Where the warrior of the flesh relies on their will and their spirit to drive them, the spiritual warrior surrenders to God's Will and therein lets the Holy Spirit be the force which drives them. They know that there is a Will and Spirit greater than anything within themselves. They also know the capabilities of that greater Spirit… their Warrior Spirit.

Torque

One of the terms we introduced above was "torque". This term is used when mechanics discuss why they go for the impact tool over another tool for a specific job, but it is also a term that is used by warriors for similar reason. I have heard Special operators described as the torque wrenches of the military.

The use of the words "turn" and "torque" are used as a play on the force which is exhibited by pneumatic, or impact, tools. This use of the word torque and its relation to impact tools, can be applied to torque and its relation to spiritual warfare. Turn is a term we know well in scripture.

Teshuvah is the Hebrew word we translate as repent, or repentance. What it means at its root is "to turn". The work of the Spirit is to turn the hearts of men toward repentance, to turn their hearts to God, to turn their hearts to Christ alone. And when we are filled with the Holy Spirit, we become that impact tool used for this purpose.

The Holy Spirit within takes us from simple humans, who by their will and spirit can use the tools they have, to warriors with the ability to live in the true concept of "turn" and "impact".

We are the vehicle upon this earth that works with maximum effect, through very little effort of our own, to provide the directed power of God to a world in need. That directed power has one result....

He is the Spirit of God which works within the hearts of others through our service to God, evangelism and prayer. And He does His work for one purpose and one purpose only...that mankind would *"Turn to Me, and be saved, all ends of the earth, For I am God, and there is none else"* (Isaiah 45:22 Young's), and *"Repent therefore, and turn again, that your sins may be blotted out, so that there may come times of refreshing from the presence of the Lord"* (Acts 3:19 WEB).

Dunamis

"that he would grant you, according to the riches of his glory, that you may be strengthened with power through his Spirit in the inward man." (Ephesians 3:16 WEB)

The Pneuma we have within, which prepares us to apply torque in our service, erupts with the power of dynamite. The Impact Warrior and Impact Prayer has a power within that detonates with a fire like no other. The pneuma applied and allowed to live within turns into something truly explosive.

The Greek word Dunamis has given us the English words dynamite and dynamic. Could you think of any two words better for the impact we are called to function in and to have upon the world around us? God's Spirit is the key to dynamic explosive dynamite power against the forces of darkness and the higher entities to which we battle.

We are not called to some feckless and impersonal power in this warfare around us. We are called to have the most effectual, almighty, and impactful power possible in this world and to apply it to the battle in which we stand.

The power God has granted unto us is a perfect power that is perfectly proportioned to the calling He has placed within us.

God describes His Spirit with dunamis, He delivers it with dunamis, He applies dunamis to all of our service in Him. Dunamis equals power…and not just any power, the almighty power of God Himself! The power of creation, the power behind all things, the ultimate and eternal power of God.

It All Adds Up

When you put together an indwelling of pneuma, coupled with the force of torque, and with the dynamic power of dunamis, it adds up to the most mind-blowing truth of scripture. God does not just call us to Himself and His service…He indwells within us and He powers our service to be all He desires.

This is where the Impact Warrior begins. Not with training, great knowledge or wisdom, not with skillsets that God seeks and needs use of. No, we can only begin to be an

Impact Warrior if God dwells within us, if His Spirit is the Warrior Spirit within. Then He will develop our skillset, He will empower our drive within, and it all adds up to us standing in warfare without fear, never alone, and always in His victory.

Warfare in the Spiritual

Warfare in the spiritual is more real than any warfare, battle or combat we could ever see or take part in here in our natural world. It is vicious in that it has effect upon the natural world without being readily seen. This is why it is of the utmost importance that we begin our discussion with the Holy Spirit.

The Holy Spirit is the IMPACT I am focusing upon in this book. Why? Because there is no other way to have impact, be an impact, or do anything impactful in the service of our God. There is no other way to function in both the supernatural and the natural, only through the Holy Spirit.

I want this to be very clear, and forward, because there are way too many today that push the Spirit to an emotional feeling, or worse to the pages of history in our faith. This is why we do not hear preachers teaching us about the power of the Spirit. Because they themselves do not know it, have never truly sought it, and they fear it when it does present itself before them and around them.

This may seem ridiculous...but it is true. The Holy Spirit has become so foreign to our comfortable Christianity that it scares us, eludes us, and therefore is misunderstood, misused, and mistakenly fit into what the world says the supernatural is.

The Holy Spirit is thought of as some Christian form of the kundalini energy of eastern mystics, it is taught as if He is the enigmatic "force" of the Star Wars universe, and I have even heard a sermon that defined the Holy Spirit as the bible's way of explaining the science of the ancient world (in the same way we try to say magik was just the science of the old world).

This is blasphemy and extremely dangerous. And, this is why the Church has lost its impact on the world around us.

The Holy Spirit is not some part of God, some magical energy that can be directed by those who have learned its ways, and He is not some higher self we are simply on the evolutionary path to become.

The Holy Spirit is God. The Holy Spirit cannot be directed by us, but He can direct us if we submit to His ways. The Holy Spirit has nothing to do with our self, and we do not evolve toward Him, we must kneel before Him.

Do you know the Holy Spirit? Do you serve with dunamis power that comes from a Spirit indwelling a surrendered heart?

IMPACT WARFARE

Core Traits

"Whosoever heareth these sayings of mine, and doeth them, I will liken him unto a wise man, which built his house upon a rock: And the rain descended, and the floods came, and the winds blew, and beat upon that house; and it fell not: for it was founded upon a rock." (Matthew 7:24-25)

Our foundation must be firmly and fully set upon Christ, upon God and no other. We have already explored the Holy Spirit and the power that comes from working in the Spirit. Now we begin building what makes the Impact Warrior unique.

God wants us to understand that we live in a world currently ruled by very unfriendly forces. That we have an adversary who stalks us like prey and who seeks our very destruction.

He wants you to know that there is a battle raging all around you in the spirit world and He desires that you live in victory, that you are an impact for His kingdom, and that you live life in the Spirit.

You may choose to ignore the conflict. You may convince yourself that you are not going to get involved at any level. You can say you just want to live your life in peace and not get involved in such things. The reality is that the powers that be either know you as theirs and therein destroy you in the schemes and plans of their war with God, or they know you as His and seek to kill and destroy you because you are part of that restraining force and hopeful light which unravels and unveils their nefarious ends.

You Are Involved

Understanding that you are involved, whether engaged or disengaged, you now have your first choice to make in this conflict, and this choice is whether to be a pawn or to be a warrior.

A warrior chooses to be involved and engaged. Once they realize and recognize there is conflict, they cannot choose not to be involved, they are not capable of being disengaged. It is almost automatic to the heart of a warrior to want to stand for what they believe in and fight to protect that which is a part of them.

When I started speaking to old friends and acquaintances, even when I thought back to my own experiences, I soon realized how true this is. When it was first known that we were needed or necessary...we were there.

Very little thought goes into the drive and decision to step up. Where the thought comes in is the logistics side of that choice. Basically, you know in an instant you are in, then the brain figures out the how.

Look at when we see emergency situations arise. There are those who instinctively jump to, assess the situation, and involve themselves in the solution or to secure the area. We see people run toward where help is needed. These are warriors.

Where can we see this in scripture, where do we see this core character of a warrior presented in those whom God calls. Isaiah chapter six is a prime example of this, and one countless ministries and Christians use to exemplify this quality. *"I heard the voice of the Lord, saying, Whom shall I send, and who will go for us? Then said I, Here am I; send me"* (Isaiah 6:8).

You see this consistently in the special forces community. When crises arise, they stand up and start gearing up before they can even be asked if they are in. When 9/11 hit, several of my contacts were in their vehicles headed to the nearest base of operations before their pagers even started beeping (yes, pagers were still high technology back then). A firefighter friend of mine stated his chief was on the phone within minutes of watching the second plane hit to volunteer his company to head up to New York and assist.

If God was to call out to you right now, if His audible voice spoke into your heart...would you go?

Do you fall into prayer without pause when you see evil at work? Does your heart and spiritual mind jump into action at the impinging of the Holy Spirit?

If you answered yes, then you have that warrior heart, that warrior mindset, and you are definitely involved. You are God's elite and you are one who is set to have impact for Christ.

Points of Ignition

Our journey into the core traits of a warrior of impact has begun. I have pointed out that simply answering the call is the first nail in the building process of a framework that we will call the Impact Warrior.

Now that we have this frame started, it is time to ignite the fire that burns within and which animates it. This is the driving core of character which defines everyone in this category of involvement.

Among Special Operators and highly trained individuals there has been identified two ignition points to the fire within. Psychologically, these core traits are the beginning of what it takes to operate at a level above the norm. When teams are looking through the ranks for those unique individuals who will get the invitation to volunteer, to take what they have to the next level, they first look for those who show what we are about to elaborate.

If you are like me, you have probably read numerous books, articles or posts that enumerate lists of what it takes to be a warrior or to be at the top of one's field. Most of these are correct, and I would agree with what they write on this topic. What I have done here is slightly different as my approach and desire is to find what all warriors have inside, not some, and which acts to ignite and fuel that fire within. From what I know and what others responded to when asked, I found these two on every list, stated in one way or another....

So, let's ignite the fire!

Unconditional Investment

"I know thy works, that thou art neither cold nor hot: I would thou wert cold or hot. So then because thou art lukewarm ... I will spue thee out of my mouth." (Revelation 3:15-16)

God does not desire wishy-washy, lukewarm Christians. Why do you think this is? Well, I will tell you it is for the same reasons that warfare in the flesh demands the same. You must be all in, or you are all out. There is no sideline bench for warriors and no recreational soldiers in this battle being waged in the spiritual realm. There are no bleachers we can stand in and just root for a side. There is only battle, and the truth is that if you are not all in then you are going to be used by the enemy for their purposes and you will find yourself on the outside. This is not a place any warrior wants to be. In fact, this is not a place any warrior would ever be found.

When I spend time with individuals at the pinnacle of elite when we speak of our armed forces, these soldiers, sailors and airmen would look at me sideways if I asked if they were all in when it comes to their service and when they go out on missions. This is unquestionable in their mind. Why would you make a choice to serve if you were not all in for the cause you believe in?

God asks the same question of all those serving in Christ. Why would you choose life and to serve your God and not be all in for what you now have been given? Why would you not be fully engaged with the one who reached in and who saved you from death and who gave you new life? Why step outside of the world and away from sin, only to dive back in or just stand by and watch it attack and destroy all that is around you? If this was going to be your choice you should have stayed where you were.

If you do not believe me, then believe Peter when he states it plainly. *"For if after they have escaped the pollutions of the world through the knowledge of the Lord and Saviour Jesus Christ, they are again entangled therein, and overcome, the latter end is worse with them than the beginning. For it had been better for them not to have known the way of righteousness, than, after they have known it, to turn from the holy commandment delivered unto them. But it is happened unto them according to the true proverb, The dog is turned to his own vomit again; and the sow that was washed to her wallowing in the mire."* (2Peter 2:20-22)

You cannot say it more clearly. Our salvation is no game and it is not to be taken lightly as some simple affair. Therefore, we must not act with abandon or carelessness. We must understand what is required of us to stand in Christ and to remain in Him always. We must learn the difference between a fair-weather Christian, and one who is reborn.

This difference is the key to every warrior who has ever lived and is the key to knowing why born-again Christians are so dangerous to the enemy. This first core trait of a warrior is that they will exhibit UNCONDITIONAL INVESTMENT.

Every moment of every day is spent invested in who they are, what they do, and who they do this for. For Christians this must be the same. We must know who we are, for we are sons and daughters of God, adopted into the family of the Living God.

You Are Born Into A Family of Warriors

Do you understand that you are a warrior now that you are in Christ? Your Father is a warrior without compare, and you are his son or daughter. This must be established in your mind and heart so that you may operate in the proper paradigm.

Would you partially invest yourself in your own family and expect great, deep returns? No, so why then would you not unconditionally invest in the family of God and live in the returns He has promised?

There is not a day that should go by without us centering ourselves and kneeling in prayer to remind ourselves of the investment we make and in the purpose to which we make it. Unconditional investment is not like investing in stocks or in a sports team we support when we have the time or the resources.

No, unconditional investment truly means we are committed no matter what the cost and at all times. We are committed without any condition having to be further met, without our investment relying on any action or cause other than what brought us to the purpose we have committed ourselves to.

I love the way that some have defined the terms unconditional & investment. *"Unconditional- not conditional or limited: Absolute"* (Merriam Webster's Dictionary). *"Investment- an act of devoting time, effort, or energy to a particular undertaking with the expectation of a worthwhile result"* (Dictionary.com). Let me put this together into one picture that speaks to all warriors, and to the impact we are here to make in battle. We give the "very" of our everything with the goal of reaching our sure victory, and all with no condition to our service as we are absolute in our pursuit and in our purpose.

But I think God has described unconditional investment for us better than we ever could define it ourselves. His definition stands to this day as our example. *"And thou shalt love the LORD thy God with all thine heart, and with all thy soul, and with all thy might. And these words, which I command thee this day, shall be in thine heart: And thou shalt teach them diligently unto thy children, and shalt talk of them when thou sittest in thine house, and when thou walkest by the way, and when thou liest down, and when thou risest up. And thou shalt bind them for a sign upon thine hand, and they shall be as frontlets between thine eyes. And thou shalt write them upon the posts of thy house, and on thy gates"* (Deuteronomy 6:5-9).

Do You Exhibit Unconditional Investment?

Extreme Motivation

So now you are all in. You have given your all, your "very", and you do not look back but only straight into the eyes of victory. Straight into the eyes of what, or who?

This is the question which demands an answer of us all when we chose to be unconditionally invested. You see our investment is in something, and it is in making that personal, deep, fully unconditional investment that we now understand what we are doing this for. For some it will be all for themselves. This is never a recipe for success and eventually will leave you in ruin, depression, and have you labelled a megalomaniac or a despot. For the warrior it is outside of themselves and it drives them in all things.

Ask any soldier, combat veteran, or warrior type that you know, and they will give you a straight answer as to their motivation. They will tell you what they were giving it all for and for what they placed it all on the line. Maybe it is for family, for country, or any number of reasons to go all in and to give your all for a cause. Whatever the motivation, what makes an impact and what makes a warrior of impact's character truly most unique is that they exhibit EXTREME MOTIVATION.

Just as with their investment which is all in and unconditional, which is not a half-hearted endeavor but one where they give all of themselves, so it is with their motivation. It is not enough to be a person who is motivated in life or who has a motivation to do a particular task or deed.

33

No, for the warrior their motivation is the absolute driving force behind every moment, every breath, and every action.

You see, the unique character trait of unconditional investment is not a single part of a warrior's make-up. It is part of an overall character that will also show a deep and driving motivation toward something, or someone. They always look onto a horizon with each mission and moment fixed upon what means most to them. And they are driven with a force of will and determination that can only be described as extreme by those who seek to understand it.

In my years in active ministry I have known countless individuals who have been invested fully and unconditionally in what they do. And if there is one area I could pinpoint where the division between being a spiritual warrior and a fanatic or zealot lies…it would be here with motivation. Just as the difference between a grounded fleshly warrior and a psychopath diverge in one's motivation for what they do in combat, so it is with Christians.

If the motivation to which you drive forward to the extreme is your ministry, your church, your programs, your impact or for what you alone can deliver to others, then you will fall into a cultic and zealot like nature. The ONLY motivation for a spiritual Christian warrior MUST be CHRIST ALONE!

With your extreme motivation set firmly upon Jesus Christ you will see your ministry succeed, your church find revival, your programs reach those most in need, and the impact you deliver to others be used of God in ways you could not have possibly imagined. A warrior's motivation is never set on the small things, not even the mid-sized things in life. A warrior sets his motivation extremely upon the ultimate of things, the prime of all parts, and therein he sees everything fit and follow in absolute magnificence.

Scripture tells it like it is, and it proclaims without hesitation on this matter; *"Let thine eyes look right on, and let thine eyelids look straight before thee. Ponder the path of thy feet, and let all thy ways be established. Turn not to the right hand nor to the left"* (Proverbs 4:25-27). The Bible sets forth what our motivation should be extremely set upon, and upon nothing else.

"Wherefore seeing we also are compassed about with so great a cloud of witnesses, let us lay aside every weight... **Looking unto Jesus the author and finisher of our faith;** *who for the joy that was set before him endured the cross, despising the shame, and is set down at the right hand of the throne of God...lest ye be wearied and faint in your minds"* (Hebrews 12:1-3 emphasis mine).

Do You Exhibit Extreme Motivation?

It's Coming Together

Upon the framework of a warrior who answers the call, who hears the voice to stand up and to serve, we have begun to see the first ignition points that kindle the raging fire within.

When you add Unconditional Investment and Extreme Motivation to a heart which has already accepted this call...you now have a warrior who will be an impact upon all he is called to and who will impact everyone and everything around them as they walk in the fire God has embraced them with.

Holding in what now burns within becomes impossible for these individuals. Jeremiah knew this and expressed this when he wrote *"Then I said, I will not make mention of him, nor speak any more in his name. But his word was in mine heart as a burning fire shut up in my bones, and I was weary with forbearing, and I could not stay"* (Jeremiah 20:9).

A warrior on fire and who now exhibits these two traits has become a force. They have become an individual who is driven and who will fight with everything they have and who will never stand down when the times call for them to stand up.

So, let's look at the impact warrior so far. What have we put together in regard to the character of an individual of such caliber:

1. They answer and respond when they hear the voice inside call out to them (the Holy Spirit). They stand without hesitation when the moment calls for action. *Do you hear God's voice asking who will go, who will stand in the gap? Have you responded to His call upon your heart? Is your answer "here am I"?*

2. They are all in. They invest themselves fully and without condition. They do not allow themselves to be part-time participants and they know there is no such thing as a spectator when the battle is on. *Do you love the Lord thy God with all of your very soul, heart*

and might? Have you invested fully in Him, holding nothing back? Are you all in?

3.   They are motivated in the extreme with their eyes firmly set upon a purpose greater than themselves. This focus on their horizon drives them with direction and is the definition to every mission, every action, and moment. *Are your eyes firmly set upon Jesus Christ? Are you focused on your many diverse operations, or are you operating solely upon where Jesus Christ is setting your course? Are you motivated by an extreme love for Jesus Christ in all you do?*

Now the fire is lit, and we can begin to see what it takes to truly have impact in our service. But these were just the underlying core character traits of a warrior. What we have discussed so far makes up the beginning and fleshes out the individual who can be identified as a warrior and whom another warrior will recognize as one of their own.

Let's next express three additional traits that I call catalysts of character. We will find the catalysts which determine the reaction of those warriors who rise to the call in war, and when the battle surrounds them.

IMPACT WARFARE

Catalysts of Character

"That he would grant you, according to the riches of his glory, that you may be strengthened with power through his Spirit in the inward man."
(Ephesians 3:16 WEB)

A Catalyst is something which triggers, initiates, or accelerates a process and/or reaction. The two core traits we elaborated in the previous chapter are in every warrior. Alone they simply make up a warrior character, but not those underpinning qualities which put that character into action.

Our reaction to stimulus is something we will speak to in a chapter ahead, but for now it is important because it is our reaction that produces action itself. This chapter is about three additional additives to the character of a warrior which get us to the Impact Warrior being framed out fully for us.

I have called these "catalysts" because to me these are seen in all warriors, a concept I am keeping to as I am not interested in what some have or exhibit... I want to put forth what is in every warrior. These catalysts though, unlike investment and motivation which operate at 100% in every warrior, are found in different proportions and quantities in each warrior and begin to create their unique form and function in Christ.

The Formula of An Impact Warrior

"For the body is not one member, but many. If the foot shall say, Because I am not the hand, I am not of the body; is it therefore not of the body? And if the ear shall say, Because I am not the eye, I am not of the body; is it therefore not of the body? If the whole body were an eye, where were the hearing? If the whole were hearing, where were the smelling? But now hath God set the members every one of them in the body, as it hath pleased him." (1 Corinthians 12:14-19)

Every warrior is unique. In special forces units this is important because they operate in small teams and they understand the strengths and weaknesses of each team member so as to build teams which complement each other in ways which lead to absolute success. God works the same. He builds His church where we each have our part and no two are exactly the same. He calls each to the strengths He gives them by His Spirit and together they make one body.

This is important as we discuss these next points in the character of the Impact Warrior. Each individual will operate in ways which are unique to their calling. Even among evangelists, no two can have the exact same delivery or approach in their ministry. When someone tries to copy or emulate someone's ministry completely, they fail because they are not working in the ministry God has given them. No, they are trying to operate in someone else's call.

The following catalysts of action will come together in the way and manner that God desires in us if we allow His Spirit to lead.

What is important to note though as we dive into this chapter is that each of these catalysts are always present in the warrior. They may have additional catalysts or traits in their character, but the two core ignitors and the three catalysts I am presenting were in every answer I received on the character of a warrior and are ones I have always seen in these individuals.

When we speak of these all coming together into a formula or recipe, we need to understand something very clearly. We, of our own will, spirit and strength, cannot follow some recipe or formula to save ourselves or to ever engage in the ministry of our desires.

This set of ingredients are used by God to create the servant with gifts He has given in the proportion He has set, and to the ministry He desires and calls us to.

I have been around many ministries and teachers who train Christians in the ways they can reach and attain the service of their heart. This can be dangerous if we are not set in our heart upon God and the Holy Spirit alone, and devoid of our personal ambitions and wants. It is very easy to become a self-help Christian and someone who teaches and preaches a self-help way to live in Christ.

I feel the need to be upfront and quite direct here…ministry, service, and living as an Impact Warrior who wields Impact Prayer to any affect in this world, and in battle, has zero self-help involved or sought, and is completely about knowing and understanding we need God-help and seeking God-help alone as our desire.

Using the Catalysts

The core traits from chapter two are built upon the Holy Spirit. Those first parts of our framework are like the skeleton of our character. The catalysts we discuss next are the framing which is structurally integral but unlike the loadbearing traits, they make up the design that God has for us.

These catalysts are much like the muscle which is what attaches to the skeleton and is what provides connectivity, range of motion, and all the action of the body.

Using the muscle analogy, we can begin to understand how they work in us and as God directs. They take our core and put it forth into reaction to the stimulus of life, survival, and battle. Just as with muscles, we need to exercise these catalysts and as we do they become stronger and their reaction more effective in the work they perform. We strengthen and exercise these markers of character through working in the service to which God calls us.

Just as a Martial Artist or Special Operator must continually work in their function to remain effective and to keep their muscles strong and properly reactive, so the Christian must operate in their calling and service to God or find these muscles in atrophy when they need them most.

An Impact Warrior lives in their calling and works always in the call of God upon their life. We need to know and really understand this so that we fuel the fires within by the action of our hearts, our minds, giving our everything for God.

So, let's discover the Catalysts of character within the Impact Warrior!

Intensity

I find it funny that when you ask the average person what life is all about, you get more answers than you could write in one book, and most are quite superficial. When I asked some of the most successful and intelligent individuals, including some of my military friends, for their answer there was one word I could use that perfectly summarizes all their statements…Intensity.

Every one of them spoke about "grabbing life by the horns", "it's about having deep moments with family", or "putting as much of yourself in every moment that life gives you". These statements directly showed an intensity that is one thing all warriors have in regard to every aspect of their life.

When they train, they do so with intensity. When they are with family, they put themselves in with intensity, when they read, intensity, when they serve, intensity. This is the theme of life for them… to do all things with intensity.

And do you know why this is so for them? Because they understand that every moment is given and to be taken for the fullest advantage it offers. No moment is deserved or guaranteed. Every single second is given to us to live, and we should live those seconds with intensity because they go as quickly as they come.

Individuals who live with an understanding of warfare, learn very quickly how fragile life is and how it can be taken in a blink of an eye. When they see this and live with this reality, they become intense. Sometimes this can be negative, and lead to many dangerous habits. But for those who have the right outlet and support, it plants them into a life that is used for all it is worth.

God calls us to live with this intensity. Scripture, and Jesus, teach us to live in the moment and to understand that this is our life, that it is short and our one chance to live it. *"Whereas ye know not what shall be on the morrow. For what is your life? It is even a vapour, that appeareth for a little time, and then vanisheth away"* (James 4:14), *"Whatsoever thy hand findeth to do, do it with thy might; for there is no work, nor device, nor knowledge, nor wisdom, in the grave, whither thou goest"* (Ecclesiastes 9:10), and *"Therefore don't be anxious for tomorrow, for tomorrow will be anxious for itself. Each day's own evil is sufficient"* (Matthew 6:34 WEB).

It Takes Intentionality to Have Intensity

So, it is not easy to live with intensity in the moment. One must be very intentional about being intense when they approach life like this. What does that mean? That means you must have a desire to be in that moment. You must treasure the moments you have in such a way that you dare not take any of them for granted. This is having the intentionality to have intensity.

When I was looking for this trait in myself, I realized how much I was taking for granted every day. Time with my kids, with my wife, even just time with God in prayer. All of it had moments I let pass and I had no real reason for letting them get by me. I was made aware of how flippant I had become when I began spending time with the warriors around me. I quickly was shocked by how intense they are, and how much life is really in them and around them.

You have to want those moments. There must be something in you that longs to have real and meaningful impact because the thought of letting the moment pass almost hurts. When I reflect on all that I know about God and intentionality, the word which came to mind was desire. So much of intensity comes from passion, and desire draws out passion in a person. If your desire is God, that will draw out your passion for God and for all His Spirit leads you in. And once that passion is directed, then intensity is released, and it becomes an ignition for so much more.

Intensity is more than just emotional moments, memories and taking the most out of life. Intensity is also about bringing the fullness of yourself into any moment.

Warriors know this precept as that is how they attack and fight in battle… with the fullness of themselves in that moment. They may use terms like ferocity, force, or severity. What they are describing is the intensity they bring to the situation and mission before them. Something else they know and understand is that such character must be directed appropriately, or it is not useful at all.

Directing our Intensity

Too often today we have intensity without direction and without control. Those two go hand-in-hand. I have seen this countless times in life and I have been told a thousand stories by combat veterans regarding this danger. You see someone who gets that look in their eye and who is seized by the moment with just a burst of unrestrained intensity. What occurs next is either tragedy, an unforgettable story, or simply a quick burn-out of that individual.

God desires that when we exhibit the character of intensity it is coupled with direction and control. How does He do this? With scripture. God has given us the law and scripture so that we may know Him wholly and that we may have His direction on our lives and the precepts of control according to His standards. Before I am ostracized by my readers here, I am not stating the law saves, nor am I saying we must follow it perfectly to keep our salvation. I am not preaching a works-based theology with this statement.

What I am setting forth is that God knew we needed direction and to understand control. He gave us His law and the pages of scripture to show us controlled and uncontrolled lives, and to exemplify for us the measure of living intensity in the person of Jesus Christ.

Do You Exhibit Intensity?

Alacrity

There are terms you do not hear often, and alacrity is one of them, but it perfectly defines and expresses this character trait. Alacrity, at its simplest, is the quality of promptness in response, and the one definition I liked the most when I heard it was that it is "putting your readiness into action".

The picture I am painting here is of character traits that come together into the package of a warrior...especially an impact warrior, one who is a driving force for the Spirit inside them.

An individual who has unconditional investment in their calling, who has extreme motivation in their service to Jesus Christ, and who lives with intensity must put all of this into action. Alacrity is that character quality of one who does not waste the moment and the intensity they have in it...they turn potential into the kinetic.

Strike While the Iron Is Hot

Something we see prevalent today that did not exist in such abundance in days long past is procrastination. In earlier times procrastination meant you starved because the crops were not planted in time or harvested timely. Procrastination meant you missed your boat, your chance, and sometimes that you would fail. Alacrity is the antithesis to procrastination.

This quality, like the others, has triggers. I liken it to the difference between a speeding ticket and a winning lottery ticket. With a speeding ticket few are in a rush to pay it and even fewer do so with any joy and anticipation to do so. Take a winning lottery ticket though and we want that paid out quickly and I am sure anyone would have a hard time hiding their joy and anticipation on receiving those winnings.

For a warrior, the joy and anticipation of service and in doing what they love is evident and very hard for them to hide. They cannot wait to channel that intensity into action, and they wait with anticipation for those moments. They are watchmen searching for when the time arrives to jump in, stand up, and to perform upon their skillset. In our everyday quips this is what is meant when we use the phrase "strike when the iron is hot".

This gives the illustration of the blacksmith waiting for the iron to reach that perfect temperature when he can strike with his hammer and beat the raw product into a useable form. It is the moment when conditions are right, and if we wait things will cool down and our actions will have no effect.

Many see this character set forth for followers of Christ in 2 Corinthians 6:1-2 we are told expressly *"Working together, we entreat also that you not receive the grace of God in vain, for he says, "At an acceptable time I listened to you, in a day of salvation I helped you." Behold, now is the acceptable time. Behold, now is the day of salvation."* (WEB)

When we hear God's directive, when the Spirit places that moment on our heart to act… we are expected to react and to go into action. An impact warrior lives his invested, motivated, intense life with readiness and eagerness to serve the Lord. This is the character of alacrity in its fullest meaning and to its fullest purpose.

A Two-Part Catalyst

Alacrity has two main components to it; one which relates to the point before we act, the other to that point once the action has been engaged in. The first is that we really understand that once opportunity presents itself, once the call demands action, once our minds are triggered, we do not procrastinate in the least, and we jump to react speedily. The second component relates to how we complete the action with the same anticipatory energy and explosive power to which we were just waiting to unleash and put forth.

The best way to have clarity when it comes to understanding alacrity is to think about how we desire God to act, and to contemplate how He reacts in scripture.

When we desire God to move in our lives and upon the lives of others we have faith that God longs to hear our prayer and for our interaction. That longing is the first component of His alacrity, as He is the father who went out to look for the prodigal to return...just as the father did not simply wait or anticipate, but actively sought to see His son, so God is active in waiting for our return and our coming before Him.

Next, once God hears the need of our heart, we desire Him to move swiftly in making the supernatural occur or the natural to take shape and accomplish what is needed and necessary in the timing as it is supposed to occur.

This is our example in regard to alacrity. We must have that anticipation to hear and seek God. We must then react without delay at the release of His Spirit and direction, in the necessary timing that God has expressed. Alacrity must move swiftly but is never haphazard. Just as God acts in perfect timing, so we must learn to anticipate His timing and act accordingly once released.

Do You Exhibit Alacrity?

Unstoppable Courage

"Be strong and of a good courage, fear not, nor be afraid of them: for the LORD thy God, he it is that doth go with thee; he will not fail thee, nor forsake thee." (Deuteronomy 31:6)

Fear is the food of that which we fight. It feeds their insatiable appetites and is the weakness most played upon with mankind. Fear is a double-edged sword as with one edge it shows we do not believe God in what He says to us and promises us, and the other edge is that we believe the entities hold more power than our God and we listen to their lies.

God understands fear better than we ever could. He knows fear and He knows the hold it has upon us and its debilitating nature. This is why God gave us the remedy for fear. He knows we will always have it and operate in some way from it. His remedy is to replace the fear which darkness uses with the fear that God alone uses...The Fear of The Lord.

This principle is used in a lesser degree within combat forces, martial artists, and elite individuals. When you train, you train to focus on the fear of failure, the fear of what happens if you do not succeed, and the fear of what will happen to all you hold dear. This drives out the fear of the enemy, the fear of death, for it is a greater fear and all lessors flee from your mind and heart.

Fear does not have to be a negative emotion or part of you. It can be positive and part of the wonder of life. When you focus on the fear of what would happen to a loved one should you fail...that fear is driven by love for them and when you focus like this those thoughts and feelings of love come forward and power that drive.

You see it on the smiling face of someone about to charge into a situation. When you ask "why the smile", they tell you they were just thinking of their daughter, their wife, or sometimes I have been surprised by the response of "I was just thinking of my dog back home". And the second that the moment they are in hits them again...the look on their face is of solid resolve and they step forward with UNSTOPPABLE COURAGE.

Fear of The Lord

The above is what the Fear of The Lord truly is. It is the awe of God that floods our minds and hearts, and which then brings forward determination and brings us into the moment with a resolve that is resolute. It grants us unstoppable courage beyond compare, and which others take notice of as unique and powerful in the warrior.

"There is no fear in love; but perfect love casteth out fear: because fear hath torment. He that feareth is not made perfect in love" (1 John 4:18). The Fear of the Lord is the

perfection of love within us. The Fear of the Lord is knowing there is no punishment for us as we are made clean by the blood of Christ. The Fear of the Lord is that awe we have for God in all He is, in all He's done, and in all He is coming to complete.

Fight On

For the warrior in the flesh, having some greater fear and the reflection on its course which brings resolve is integral to showing that remarkable courage which we, especially Americans, love to applaud and to reward in others. For the spiritual warrior, having the Fear of the Lord brings us determination in His promises, knowledge in the truth which sends all lies to flight, and which becomes a resolve greater than any darkness can destroy or defeat.

The definition of unstoppable is quite simple and direct; "incapable of being stopped" (Merriam-Webster). This character trait is necessary for all the others to come together in working order and to produce the impact warrior of affect. This trait is the sheeting which surrounds the framework and provides the shell and stabilization to hold together as one the character we have which contains the fire of God within. This courage we operate in is unstoppable because the force within and behind it is God Himself and no other. We have framed our being, our very life and self around and upon the person of almighty God.

Because we have ourselves immersed in God, we can have nothing less than impact, and be nothing less than an impact, on everything and everyone around us. This is what others see and what we can define as the strength in the face of pain and obstacle. This is what we can define as action in the presence of that which frightens. This is what will be described as courage...and courage which by its design now is incapable of ever being stopped.

It is important that you understand the importance of operating in this level of unstoppable courage. This is where God expects and calls us to. This is the deep waters that would frighten others, but, where we do not swim...we walk upon.

Do You Exhibit Unstoppable Courage?

The Framework and The Fire

Can you see these catalysts of character in yourself? Do you see them in those you know are spiritual warriors of the faith? Do you desire to exhibit these and work in these to where they become the framework of your character as an Impact Warrior?

Let's look at the Impact Warrior again. This time we need to look at this structure and fire and see it as the base for a life only God can write and empower. We need to take these and make them real in our life and become the basis for our service to God. We must have the Holy Spirit and these core character traits within us so that we may engage fully in the battle, as we will discuss in the next chapters.

We must then have and exercise the catalysts in this chapter to bring action to our character. So, let's go over all of the points from chapter one, two and three that we have been presented with. Let's flesh out the character and action, before we delve into the battle:

1.   The Holy Spirit is the force within us, and which drives us. The Holy Spirit takes us from having some effect, into being Impact Warriors who are used to maximize effect, and which deliver maximum torque with minimal exertion by us. *Do you have the Holy Spirit working within you? Have you responded to Christ and received the power of the Holy Spirit that we are promised as believers in Christ?*

2.   Impact Warriors answer and respond when they hear the voice inside call out to them. They stand without hesitation when the moment calls for action. *Do you hear God's voice asking who will go, who will stand in the gap? Have you responded to His call upon your heart? Is your answer "here am I"?*

3.   Impact Warriors are all in. They invest themselves fully and without condition. They do not allow themselves to be part-time participants and they know there is no such thing as a spectator when the battle is on. *Do you love the Lord thy God with all of your very soul, heart and might? Have you invested fully in Him, holding nothing back? Are you all in?*

4.   Impact Warriors are motivated in the extreme with their eyes firmly set upon a purpose greater than themselves. This focus on their horizon drives them with direction and is the definition to every mission, every action, and moment. *Are your eyes firmly set upon Jesus Christ? Are you focused on your many diverse operations, or are you operating solely upon*

where Jesus Christ is setting your course? Are you motivated by an extreme love for Jesus Christ in all you do?

5.   Impact Warriors have passion that produces intensity and they live lives of intensity in all they do. This is intentional and directed as they place the fullness of themselves in the fullness of each moment. *Do you live with yourself fully operating in the moment? Do you have a passion for God that burns with intensity?*

6.   Impact Warriors operate with alacrity and live to put their readiness and eagerness into action. They do not hesitate nor procrastinate when the moment calls for action. *Do you serve God with alacrity? Do you wait in eager anticipation for those times when we are called to act?*

7.   Impact Warriors have unstoppable courage and resolve. They know the Fear of the Lord and they function at the highest levels of courage as they step out and stand up with no fear. *Do you Fear the Lord and walk in His Spirit? Do you step out into the deep where others are frightened to go and serve?*

We now know the makings of an Impact Warrior's character and action. We have discussed in part some of the obstacles and warfare that spiritual operators must serve in.

NOW, prepare to be geared up, trained up, and to stand up!

IMPACT WARFARE

Gear Up to Stand Up

"Wherefore take unto you the whole armour of God, that ye may be able to withstand in the evil day, and having done all, to stand." (Ephesians 6:13)

Are you starting to feel like a warrior? Reading the first few chapters are you starting to see the warrior within you and that you are? Are you beginning to see that we are not called to a casual stroll with Jesus, that this is a walk through the battlefield of this world in active warfare?

That thought can be overwhelming for some and a bit much to grasp. It is not meant to be though. For you see the gospel message is that Jesus Christ has already claimed the victory and set us free! The Holy Spirit now resides within you and God is equipping you first, and foremost, with

Himself before all else we are about to break down in this chapter.

The Holy Spirit is the indwelling "warrior spirit" within the Impact Warrior. The Spirit is the breath of each heartbeat and the dynamic, explosive power that ignites the core traits forming the base of every warrior. Upon this base a framework takes shape comprised of individually developed levels of essential catalysts that fuel, direct, and become the vehicles for the fire within. All of this is the Warrior for Christ, one who is solely focused on the call and commission of Jesus and who…above all else…stands up!

It is time to prepare the warrior for combat, the environment he is designed to operate within. Our calling is not to sit in weighted anticipation motionless and in silence while the world spins and time passes. No, we are called to action and to proclaim the gospel message. We are called to stand up and step out…and this can only be done if we have the equipment, the protection, and the tools necessary and needed.

I find it noteworthy that when Paul expounds on the armor of God, he states the verb "to stand" several times. This is not done without great knowledge of the warrior mind and life. For there is a very good reason that warriors stand tall in war, walk with shoulders square at the front, and stride with confidence during times of chaotic frenzy and disarray. It is because they know what they are capable of and trust their gear intrinsically. They are secured in the power behind them and by the equipment they wear and wield, and it gives them the ability to focus on the task at hand without needing to worry that they are protected and ready for all that may come their way.

Not a Costume or Casual Outfit

The warrior does not wear his gear, or given armor, casually…unless he desires to end up a casualty! This is no mere costume to pretend to put on and to play soldier in. This is real combat dress meant for one purpose, and one purpose only: warfare.

When I trained in combat readiness it was always drilled into me the importance of one's equipment. The protective gear you wear into battle is what protects your vital organs and fragile body so that you live to fight another day. Wearing one piece wrong, forgetting any part, could be detrimental and cost you your life, or leave you maimed. Equipment checks are not only done when donning this gear…it is checked, adjusted, and fastened tight each and every moment one catches their breath and has the opportunity.

Likewise, we should be taking up and placing on the Armor of God at the start of every day. Then as we progress through our day, we should be stopping to take stock of where we are, check our gear to make sure we have kept it secure and tight to our person, and we should adjust accordingly, as needed. Life can be chaotic and fast paced, it is the duty of a warrior to stop, breathe, and find the time necessary to perform an equipment check, take a breath, and to get their bearings.

Let me be clear on something here. You will never succeed and be effective, you will never have the impact that God desires, if you do not perform self-care and from time-to-time set yourself apart and do what was just discussed. Breath, pray, re-orient and get your bearings, refresh and get back out there. Even Jesus would set Himself apart at times for this purpose. This practice will ensure you stay focused, never let your guard and gear down, and that you are always prepared for the next assault or adventure around the corner.

Something I have always found impressive is how elite combat warriors know their equipment. I mean every strap is checked; every stitch tested. They ensure it is not only functional, but that it is ready to take the force of battle so that they do not have to. A lot of faith is placed in this equipment.

Christians are not so thorough in checking their equipment. As a point of fact, when I ask the average Christian to enumerate the armor and weapons that God has given us in life and to be effective in our battle... sadly only around seventy percent even know what I am talking about. And of those, maybe ten percent can mention them all correctly.

Paul tells us very clearly that the armor we are given, the equipment and weapons of our warfare, are so that we can do two things above all else. They are to give us the ability to withstand evil when it comes against us, and to stand after the battle is past.

This is the same with the gear of modern warfare, and what every warrior places faith in...that their armor and gear will allow them to withstand the rigors of combat, and that when all is said and done, they walk off the battlefield standing tall.

The question one should be asking then, is why do so few Christians know their gear, their equipment, what they are called to don so that they can withstand and stay standing through all life and the entirety of darkness that evil will throw their way?

More Than a Prayer

Every Christian who knows the details of Ephesians chapter six should know that this was not written so that we could recite it as a prayer each morning, or throughout the day, with the expectation this alone protects us and equips us.

This is not to say that prayer of this nature and as remembrance is wrong...by no means is this true. What this means is that we are to actually use this training to gear up and to stand up. We should go through each article and place it as directed, check that it fits, and walk knowing it is in place serving its intended purpose.

Let me explain how this operates, and how every day warriors use the same practice in what they do to prepare for battle and combat. When you go through training, they drill into you the mental checklists of what it takes to have success in combat. They make you gear up, tear down, gear up, tear down...it is repeated over and over again during the training phase of a soldier. This is done so that you eventually have repeated it enough times that the memorization allows you to mentally prepare and go through each step to ensure no article, part or piece is missed or out of place.

This would allow us to mentally close our eyes and go through each step visually preparing while we geared up and checking each piece as it was applied. No single item or article was missed, because you knew it as imperative for it all to be there and to be placed as intended. Ephesians is designed for this same purpose and application. Properly understood and utilized, we can visually prepare and functionally apply God's armor daily without missing any piece, without any item not being properly applied to its designed purpose.

It is my belief that this is what the Holy Spirit, through Paul, had planned with these verses. They are there for us to memorize and to become the mnemonic device for our preparedness and ability to apply the gear of battle. Our prayer should be for the express purpose of visually gearing up, applying our given armor and weapons, and standing in Christ.

Application of God's Armor

We must now learn about each part of the armor of God, and how to apply it to our person so that we may stand in battle and have the impact God desires.

To begin, this is not our armor this is *God's* armor… "the whole armor of God". We know this as God bears this armor upon Himself as we see in Isaiah 59:17.

The Holy Spirit gives us this armor, is the power behind this armor, and is the power behind the weapons we are given in this warfare.

We have the indwelling Spirit, we have set Christ alone as our rock and salvation, we exhibit the character traits and catalysts of an Impact Warrior...now we work in the Spirit to gear up and stand up.

We will break down all seven individual pieces of armor and weaponry that Paul enumerates in Ephesians six. And yes, though many may teach differently, there are seven very distinct and individual parts to this armor and weaponry, not six.

Paul illustrates wonderfully for us this truth as he was given understanding based on what he knew and saw every day in the typical armed Roman soldier, and from the vision in Isaiah.

So, let's stand in the entire applied armor of God!

The Belt of Truth

"Stand therefore, having your loins girt about with truth" (Ephesians 6:14)

In ancient times, and still today in some cultures, the belt wrapped around one's waist was not to simply hold up your pants. It was usually broader in width and was an integral part of fastening oneself and one's attire. For the warrior it acted to increase inter-abdominal pressure, to stabilize one's spine, provide for a strong core, and to help increase the maximum power exerted. This principle use for a belt is what lies behind the utility belts and lifting belts used in sports and the trades today.

Prepare and Strengthen Oneself

The phrase "gird up your loins" has always meant to prepare and to strengthen oneself for hard work or battle.

Warfare is as intense an activity as anyone could find themselves in. The forces exerted upon the physical, mental and emotional are enormous. God knows this, and so tells us to begin by preparing and strengthening ourselves...and not with just any belt material, but with a belt whose material makeup is truth itself.

"I am the Way, the Truth, and the Life" (John 14:6)

Jesus Christ is the truth. What does that mean? It means that He is the belt which secures so that our covering does not slip, fail, or fall away. He is that covering by His shed blood and He secures us firmly so that maximum power may be exerted in His name. And what is this maximum power...well, we have already shown it is the Holy Spirit.

I have always thought of the Holy Spirit as the most integral part of this Belt of Truth, He is the buckle which locks the belt in place and keeps it firmly secured.

We know from John 14:17 that the Holy Spirit is also known as the "Spirit of Truth". And we also know that the indwelling Holy Spirit is set as a seal upon the salvation that Jesus Christ secured; *"that ye heard the word of truth, the gospel of your salvation: in whom also after that ye believed, ye were sealed with that holy Spirit of promise"* (Ephesians 1:13). The Holy Spirit seals and sets firmly in the most unbreakable way, the Belt of Truth that girds our loins.

As we read in some of the English versions of Ephesians 6:14, they use terms such as buckled and fastened to translate the Greek word used by Paul, *perizosamenoi*. These are fair modern words for "gird", and for me sets the interpretation of the Holy Spirit as that fastener of truth which is Christ in us.

The Application of Truth

Secure yourself in the truth that Jesus Christ is your salvation, and rest in the truth that this salvation is locked in place by the Holy Spirit. This is our preparation for warfare, and the beginning of our bearing and standing in the armor of God.

Jesus Christ has covered us and then He Himself has wrapped us in His truth so that in Him this covering cannot slip, fail, fall, or become displaced...and this is buckled and fastened by nothing less than the Holy Spirit which seals us into the truth!

This is also how the Belt of Truth becomes a weapon and not just armor. All of God's armor has protective application, both defensive and offensive. If we are wrapped in truth, others will see our fortitude and the firmness in which we stand. We will stand with the posture of truth and others will take notice.

A strong core is one of the secrets behind the best warriors who make it a point of constant training to position their core and to develop their core for the delivery of maximum force. The Belt of Truth, and living in truth, develops our core in the same way. It makes us a powerhouse and impact like nothing else.

The Breastplate of Righteousness

"...*having on the breastplate of righteousness*" (Ephesians 6:14)

The breastplate is designed as a heavy protection over the vital organs of the body. It must be able to take the blunt force of a weapon so that you do not have to. There are many organs protected by the breastplate, but probably the most important is the heart... "*That he would grant you, according to the riches of his glory, to be strengthened with might by his Spirit in the inner man; That Christ may dwell in your hearts by faith*" (Ephesians 3:16-17).

Scripture tells us to "*Guard our heart with diligence*" (Proverbs 4:23). This is why we must allow Christ to reign upon the throne of our heart, so that what flows forth is of God and not of the ways or desires of mankind or the world.

Once Jesus Christ reigns in our heart, our heart will become a target of the enemy. This is why the breastplate is the next piece we put into its place. The moment we embrace and are girded in truth, Satan will attack the heart as it is the next target of opportunity.

Our heart is the foundation of our emotional response and is easily attached to others in negative and positive ways. And so now Satan chooses the powerful arrows of greed, adultery, envy, rage, and more, which all target the soft hearts of men. But when we seat Christ firmly in the heart and apply His righteousness as the breastplate of God's armor...Satan soon finds an impenetrable covering.

The Application of Righteousness

What is righteousness, and how can it be a breastplate which protects our heart and the vital organs of our life and faith?

Righteousness is the quality of being right in the eyes of God. This is not possible for us, at all. Contrary to what many religions and bible teachers will tell you, there is absolutely no way for us to be accounted righteous through our own works and deeds. Our righteousness comes squarely from Jesus Christ and the indwelling Holy Spirit. Our faith in God, and in the work of Jesus Christ alone in our atonement, is accounted unto us as righteousness (see Romans 4:3).

"For he hath made him to be sin for us, who knew no sin; that we might be made the righteousness of God in him." (2 Corinthians 5:21).

So, how do we apply to our protection the Breastplate of Righteousness? It would not seem enough to just have Jesus in your heart, and how can this be a weapon in our warfare?

Psalm 119:10-11 gives us the psalmists understanding of applying this in our life when he wrote *"With my whole heart have I sought thee: O let me not wander from thy commandments. Thy word have I hid in mine heart, that I might not sin against thee."* It is not for us to simply just apply righteousness, we are to seek it continually.

If we are seeking Christ, and to place Him on our heart, continually…then we are not seeking after the world and sin. We no longer are tempted by the sins of the heart because we have a new heart focused on one thing alone…Jesus.

Jesus in our heart does not make us perfection in righteousness, but it is perfect righteousness that protects our heart and its integrity for combat.

This is a weapon much like the Belt of Truth, it makes us a beacon of something different and opposed to this world and to Satan. This makes the breastplate a psychological weapon, if you will, which undermines the lies and the sin that Satan has convinced the world is happiness and the fulfillment of the heart.

This is why some versions of Ephesians use the terminology "arrayed" when it speaks of how the Breastplate of Righteousness is placed. I believe this is because they understand that we are to display this piece of armor and let others see it upon us. This is how it becomes a weapon against this world.

The Footwear of the Gospel

"...your feet shod with the preparation of the gospel of peace" (Ephesians 6:15)

Our belt is firmly fit, the breastplate secured upon our body, we now are ready to go forth into battle. To move forward in our mission, we must understand the means and medium which covers our feet.

Our feet must be protected from the sharp traps and brokenness of this world which would seek to cut them up and to slow our progress. To protect our stride and set our feet upon their course, we fit our feet with the preparation of the Gospel.

Romans 10:15 asks the question, "*And how shall they preach, except they be sent? as it is written, How beautiful are the feet of them that preach the gospel of peace, and bring glad tidings of good things!*" God knows that we must have protections to move in our calling, and so the very Gospel of Christ becomes the footwear of protection. It is the answer to every obstacle and slippery slope we face as we move forward in Christ.

The Application of the Gospel

One of the items which made the roman soldiers so unstoppable was the effectiveness of their footwear. They could march for hours and miles without fear their feet would get cut or that they would have to walk upon sharp stones. It allowed them to walk upon any road, and to grip the ground for sure footing when needed. This made them an army on the march, and which could march anywhere and through anything.

The Romans were feared, as was any army whose soldiers could march and fight with sure feet and traction. We are also feared by this same rationale. We march in unison to the beat of a cadence set by God and with surety of each step and firmness of each footfall.

This is what the gospel is for us. If we apply the Gospel message as the platform upon which we stand and move, we will find our footing secured and each step sure along the way. The Gospel will keep us from slipping, keep us from being cut or effected by the sharp brokenness around us. And as we stride about the brokenness and rugged terrain of this world the Gospel is a weapon against lies and deceit.

The Gospel dispels all that Satan has convinced the world is truth. It shows that no matter the obstacles or shattered pieces which lie sharply before us, they have an antidote and a solution.

The Gospel is our commission, our greatest call is to go forth in the Gospel and with the Gospel.

With our feet shod and protected they become a very real weapon for us to use in combat. We can navigate with flexibility and we are able to run into combat without delay or worry of the path before us.

The Shield of Faith

"...*taking the shield of faith, wherewith ye shall be able to quench all the fiery darts of the wicked*" (Ephesians 6:16)

With our armor secured upon our body, with our feet prepared to go forward, we now grab for our shield which quenches the fiery darts of the Devil and his schemes of darkness that are flying toward us.

Satan knows we now have truth, so he attacks the heart; we have God's Righteousness protecting the heart so he makes sure the brokenness of the world impedes our steps; we have the shoes of the Gospel to prepare our way and cover our steps so that we now move forward...so Satan launches his artillery through the air meant to knock us to the ground.

Our faith, set firmly around us and before us, now becomes a mighty shield that deflects and keeps the sharp points and burning fire of Satan's attack from ever making contact. He cannot knock us off our feet, for the Shield of Faith takes upon itself the force of his attack.

The Application of the Shield of Faith

Faith is not meant to be stored away or kept secret, hidden from view. No, faith is a mighty sign and armor which when placed upon our arm and used for its intended purpose creates an impenetrable buttress against the darkness that presses so forcibly upon us. And this is how faith becomes a weapon as well as an armament; in that we, by faith, can press against the enemy with great force, knowing we are safe from the long and short ranged weapons of evil.

"Now faith is the substance of things hoped for, the evidence of things not seen." (Hebrews 11:1). Faith is active and is evident. Faith has substance and is the power behind things seen and unseen. One's faith is the belief in the evident presence and reality of their hope...and for the Impact Warrior of God, that hope is Jesus Christ and the very promises of almighty God.

Satan attacks our faith by questioning our belief in God, our belief in His promises, and by firing his next weapon of choice...doubt.

Doubt is the most powerful weapon against God's shield which is about us. Watering down our faith, twisting our faith, and confusing our faith work to drop our shield or for us to not use this armor to its greatest potential and protective / offensive means.

As we have seen with the progression thus far, God next equips us with the proper protection against all that Satan now will direct against the mind and faith of the warrior of God, the Warrior of Impact who is striding forcibly into the world with great effectiveness.

The Helmet of Salvation

"...*and take the helmet of salvation*" (Ephesians 6:17)

Doubt and confusion are attacks against the mind. They target the one part of our body which may find itself becoming exposed as we peek around the shield to see and navigate the road we press on and the line we press against. This target is also critical to bring down the shield which we place so strongly against Satan.

Therefore, God has now given us a helmet to place upon our head and to protect our mind from these new devices turned against us.... This helmet and head covering are nothing less than our very salvation itself.

You may ask, how is our salvation a protective helmet against the attacks of doubt and confusion? Well, it is the assuredness of salvation, the work of our salvation, and the seal of our salvation upon our head which makes it such a powerful weapon and protective piece of equipment in our arsenal.

The Application of the Helmet of Salvation

The mind is a vulnerable and easily tricked organ. It is swayed by all the senses, and is the source of all thought, reason and intelligence. So, these are the attacks that Satan uses and which the helmet is placed to protect.

"Casting down imaginations, and every high thing that exalteth itself against the knowledge of God, and bringing into captivity every thought to the obedience of Christ" (2 Corinthians 10:5)

This is how the helmet of God...the Helmet of Salvation works. By setting without doubt in our minds that Christ's working of our salvation was complete, eternal, and enough. A mind set firmly upon the truth and the salvation of Jesus resting therein tears apart all attacks that Satan would fire at our mind.

We must take captive our running thoughts, we must hold up all argument to the light, we must grab hold of all running ideas and temptations and bring them against the full weight and work of Jesus Christ.

From this we now have a most effective weapon in that our minds are not easily swayed, our thoughts are not tossed about like a rudderless ship upon the waves of a turbulent sea (James 1:6) ... no, we are steadfast in our conviction and a lighthouse to all those ships around us.

With the Helmet of Salvation in its place and our armor fully secured and used in its full intended use, we are a force and a power like no other on this earth.

Now with darkness stopped in its tracks and its weapons nullified, we wield the impact weapons which fight it back, steal its territory, and which have great effect for this world and for those living in darkness.

The Sword of the Spirit

"...and the sword of the Spirit, which is the word of God"
(Ephesians 6:17)

The Sword of the Spirit is a mighty and potent weapon when wielded rightly and in the Spirit. *"For the word of God is quick, and powerful, and sharper than any two-edged sword, piercing even to the dividing asunder of soul and spirit, and of the joints and marrow, and is a discerner of the thoughts and intents of the heart."* (Hebrews 4:12)

This is no ordinary sword which we are granted permission to carry into battle. This is the very Word of God which rightly divides, and which is the antithesis and opposition to all the weapons which Satan has in his limited arsenal. Satan's sword is a twisted version of the true word of God and one which is quickly, and easily, seen as a counterfeit and as inferior in the presence of the true Sword of the Spirit.

The Application of the Sword of the Spirit

The Sword of the Spirit is applied to attack the powers of darkness by shining light upon them. The sword must be something we constantly train with, sharpen, and keep polished. When we speak of warriors, whether from ancient times or modern day, their weapon is always kept with the greatest of care and with doting diligence.

Never can it become rusty, dull, or be left to decay and crumble with the tarnish and grime of time. If a warrior left his weapon to sit and collect dust, they would find it unable to be effective when needed, and too weighty to handle with ease when necessary.

When I have trained with special operators, they use their weapons and train with them almost daily. They know that they must never take for granted that it will work and not malfunction when lives are on the line. In like manner, we must daily train with our weapon and hone our skill in its use so that when lives are on the line it is ready and masterfully wielded.

Satan is only able to twist the Word and defeat our handling of the Sword of the Spirit, when we have taken for granted that we know it as well as we can and that there is nothing new to learn of it. When we feel we have mastered it, we must keep at it continually as any true master knows that mastery comes only from familiarity and intimate regular knowledge.

When was the last time you read God's Word? When was the last time you went to recall a scripture and misquoted or mis-cited it, even if slightly? I promise you that Satan knows these answers, and his forces pay close attention to how you train in the Word.

Armor is essential to withstanding the full attacks levied against us in battle, but we are useless in combat if we cannot manage and hold back evil and thwart its nefarious plans and schemes. And know that we shall face attack and outright warfare the moment we are His, the moment we stand in Christ, the moment He calls us to preach the Gospel and to the commission we have to make disciples and to baptize in His name.

The Sword of the Spirit is a weapon without equal for its purpose and in our calling, but it is not our only weapon. For a sword is a close quarter weapon which has its limits, and which is limited in its ability to work beyond the wielder. For this purpose, Paul ends by elaborating on our final piece in the Armor of God, the long range and immensely destructive weapon, which is launched by us, but which is solely the direct, and directed, power of the Holy Spirit!

Prayer in the Spirit

"*Praying always with all prayer and supplication in the Spirit, and watching thereunto with all perseverance and supplication for all saints*" (Ephesians 6:18)

We will focus intensely upon prayer in part two of this book, but it must be mentioned here as it is part of the Armor of God.

Just as Satan has fiery darts and long-term assault weapons that he uses against us, so God has the ultimate long-range weapon which is His presence and power manifest in His personal action upon petition and through direct communication and supplication of His children.

Prayer can move beyond walls, across oceans, and can speak into time and space. Prayer may intercede, it may seek direction, and it most importantly keeps us aligned and moving at all times in the Spirit.

As stated, we will go greatly into detail in future chapters on application of prayer and understanding of its purpose and power. For this chapter it is important to relate it to the spear, the pilum or javelin, of the roman soldier. This most precious weapon kept the enemy at a distance to control the battle. This weapon could be thrown to take down an enemy long before they were close enough to be a threat. This weapon was seen by the enemy and worked to thwart the plans for attack by sheer intimidation and knowledge of how effective this weapon is in the hands of one skilled in its use.

Therefore, prayer is often attacked by Satan through distraction, through making our schedules so busy that we have no time to grow in our use of it. This is why Satan attacks how we use it and works to make it ineffective through unfamiliarity and sheer failure to ever learn its true power.

For the power of prayer lies in its ability to take power from the darkness, to bind it and remove it from the battlefield before it even has the chance. Prayer removes the sting and fangs of our foe and it can protect others, fight for others, and it can change the atmosphere and destroy the strongholds of even the most entrenched enemy forces. Prayer brings the living God into the battle, and His victory is not only complete, but it decimates the ranks of all those who stand against Him and His!

In Conclusion

As an Impact Warrior we stand, and we eagerly prepare and are ready for battle. Filled with the Holy Spirit we now gear up as He directs so that we withstand all that comes against us and stand at the end of every battle.

The Armor of God is nothing less than God Himself placed upon us and given to us for protection and to accomplish our calling and to fight in this war.

Did you notice something very interesting as we enumerate and elaborate upon the seven individual parts Paul gives us in Ephesians? Each, and every piece is an illustration of how Jesus Christ is to be applied to our life and our walk.

Jesus is the truth, and therein He is the belt of truth that girds our loins and secures our core.

Jesus is our righteousness, and therein He is our breastplate which guards the heart.

The Gospel is Jesus Christ, and therein He has shod our feet and steadied our walk in His commission.

Our faith is in Jesus Christ, our hope, and therein he shields us from the assault of Satan's fiery darts.

Jesus is our salvation, and therein He is the helmet that protects our mind and guards our thoughts from evil.

Jesus is the Word, and therein He is the sword which we wield to defeat the darkness around us.

Jesus taught us to pray and He intercedes for us, and therein He is the power which breaks strongholds.

We began by stating that we serve Jesus Christ alone and we are Impact Warriors because we have set Jesus Christ alone as our everything. We have given ourselves to the indwelling of the Holy Spirit which is the power and the presence of God within us. It is Jesus and our searching for

Him in our all, it is the Spirit which we seek in our all, that has provided and provisioned all.

Jesus Christ is our purpose and our conviction, and when we give ourselves to Him completely, He sets Himself as the armor and the weapons of our battle. And why does He do this? Because He has already claimed victory, He has already defeated our enemy and the darkness in which it lives. He calls us, and He equips us for the mission and life of following Him in this war.

IMPACT WARFARE

Reaction, Response & Perspective

"be not afraid of their terror, neither be troubled; But sanctify the Lord God in your hearts: and be ready always to give an answer to every man that asketh you a reason of the hope that is in you with meekness and fear." (1 Peter 3:14-15)

An Impact Warrior set in the Holy Spirit, with their heart and mind firmly in Christ, their character traits fleshed out, and their gear/armor in place, can be the most feared and fearsome answer to the evil we know works in this world today. Yes, they *can be*... but that does not mean that they always are.

Our reaction and response is just as important as anything we have discussed so far. Eyes are always upon us, physical and spiritual, to see how we react and respond to darkness and our calling as we walk with God. You can be the most grounded warrior, with the armor fully applied, but if you respond and react poorly this is all anyone will see and know of the message you bring forward. Our action brings definition to what we preach, and God always asks us to answer with meekness, gentleness, understanding, respect, fear, and humility in all we do.

This is not easily done. In-fact, this may be the toughest ask that God places upon us. Or so many of us would think. But the more you know and live a warrior's life, the more you become confident in the power you have, that you represent, and in the gear and equipment you are given, the more you naturally have a measured reaction and response to everything that occurs to you and around you in this world.

This is what God desires, that we react and respond from a place of wisdom, respecting His power as well as those we may wield it against. When we go forth in the impact, we must learn that impact is both decisive and divisive in its power and its outcome when applied. Impact though does not always mean destruction, nor does it mean we just tear into things and render them undone.

Going back to an earlier illustration, imagine you went to your mechanic to get your tires rotated and in removing your tires he had difficulties, so he broke off the wheel studs and severely damaged the wheel hub assemblies. When you see the damages listed that needed repair, and the hefty bill, he states "well the lug nuts just did not want to come off, so I grabbed my impact tools and I got those tires off and rotated them for you as you asked. I had to get the job done".

Would you think his reaction and response to the problem was measured and appropriate? I wonder if your reaction and response back would be measured as well?

As an Impact Warrior you will come against contrived difficult obstacles, obstinate and obtuse individuals, deliberate obfuscation... and an improper reaction and unmeasured response is exactly what Satan desires. He wants nothing more than to pull you from your security in Christ and to make you a banner for his campaign. He wants others to see your reaction and response and for it to dull the light and water down the salt of our calling to this world. He wants your reactions and responses as you try to fulfill the calling God asks of you in these circumstances to appear as unmeasured and irrational as the mechanic in our illustration.

Does this mean that our reaction and response will never cause damage, never be strong and direct, never be to tear something down such as a stronghold? Not at all. What this means is that when a response of great strength and possible ferocity is required it is done in measured congress with the Holy Spirit, with a heart and mind in Christ, and measured to meet the proper reply and desired action of God.

We see this principle at work in the response of Jesus to the money changers in John 2:13-17 and to the calling of Jeremiah "*See, I have this day set thee over the nations and over the kingdoms, to root out, and to pull down, and to destroy, and to throw down, to build, and to plant*" (Jeremiah 1:10). Our response must be appropriate to the desired effect and with the desired affect that God desires.

As a warrior, engaged in active warfare that changes in seconds and requires reactions at times with lightening speed, training in measured and controlled reactions and response is crucial. If one reacts too quickly, or too slowly, and responds incorrectly to the situation...then trouble will ensue, or the entire mission can be compromised.

When I have trained with special operators and spent time with them, they introduced me to a concept and training that they use to shorten reaction time and allow for the controlled and timely response that is adequate to whatever cause or case to which it is applied. And, the more I studied and applied this concept to myself and to active spiritual warfare and ministry...I found it not only fully applicable and adequate, but it has tempered my deportment and allowed me to overcome some of the issues I have had in the past, especially in my youth, with emotional responses and petty reactions.

This is not some magical formula, though it is formulaic in its structure. It takes intentional use to get better at using this tool and making it a part of your "muscle memory" if you will in the spiritual warfare we face. This concept takes already understood triggers and our stimulus response to direct all reactive response to be timely, measured, yet fire with lightning speed.

The O.O.D.A. Loop*

The OODA loop is a concept that can be applied to the combat operations process and was formulated by the late Colonel John Boyd USAF (1927-1997). The OODA loop is a cycle which was conceptualized and developed to train personnel to handle complex and complicated reactions and response. The loop must first be identified and understood, and from there it is practiced to better process through the loop with faster and more detailed responses.

To put it plainly, the faster one can process the loop, the better the ability to react and respond in the measured way that a soldier or warrior would be required to act. This process was devised by Colonel Boyd originally for pilots of advanced fighter aircraft who must operate in dogfights and at breakneck speeds where such mastery of reaction and response is required. They act just as fast as the threat comes upon them and with the outcome being that the multi-million-dollar aircraft returns to base with the pilot alive and mission complete.

Imagine for a second that you are travelling at mach speeds, with targets that are engaged at that speed and/or are themselves travelling at mach speeds against you as their target. Decisions and results will happen at this intense pace and the requirements upon the pilots are the very epitome of intense.

Now you can begin to see how this process can benefit and be critical to almost any circumstance, any platform and work across any sphere, specialty or vocation to improve the decisions we make and the energies we direct. If this is effective for our top fighter pilots and special operation forces, then it is proven by the toughest environment and by top tier individuals.

OODA is an acronym which identifies the four main parts in this process; **Observe-Orient-Decide-Act**. These have been identified as present when all individuals process stimulus that has been applied or engaged. These four parts make up the process as it relates to reaction time as expressed in the following formula:

Human Reaction Time = Time Elapsed between Onset of Stimulus and the Onset of Response.

When a stimulus is applied, we first observe it, then we orient ourselves toward it, we decide what to do based upon it, and we act accordingly. This is gone through over, and over again until we develop a faster and faster loop through them. As we develop this process, we can apply it to all stimuli and to all everyday decision making.

For an Impact Warrior engaged in spiritual warfare…this process and the understanding of it are essential to ensuring that the power God gifts to us and which flows through us becomes applied to maximum effect and in the spirit of impact to which we are called. It gives us the control so that we never blindly apply His power and we never react and respond in a way which does not bring glory to God, nor detract from His Glory.

So, let's go through each of these four steps in the process and understand their application and how to train ourselves for maximum warfare impact.

Observe

"Seeing many things, but thou observest not" (Isaiah 42:20)

It would seem simple enough to start with observation, but you would be naïve to think we observe much of what occurs around us, and to us, each day. When you are actually trained to observe or begin to truly pay attention to the world around you, you find out quickly how much of your life, and the lives of those around us, are set on autopilot.

In a world filled with distraction this first step to master this loop finds us having to be observant. God also calls us to be observant in life and in the warfare we live in. Observation means we are aware, we are awake, and we are mindful of the fact that this world is always moving, always stimulating, and always ready to throw a million different things at us.

The trick to being observant is that we are seeking. For the Christian this is part and parcel of the call on our heart...to be always seeking God. Seeking means we are seeing, paying attention means we are observant and therein not missing what matters. I like to express this when I teach as our opportunity to see God moving and working in all things because for the first time, we desire to see Him and so we desire to watch and to observe with open eyes and childlike anticipation for every place that He will choose to be seen.

In the military they have a term for when we are supposed to pay careful attention and to ensure we observe all around us..." keep your head on a swivel". This means to be constantly on the lookout and paying attention to what is all around you with intent. At any given moment an enemy can choose to engage, or a trap might be set against us. The observant warrior is seldom surprised, because they are always looking and searching the environment around them for any sign of what is around or that may be on the horizon. Sounds much like what we see in the character of a prophet...perhaps that is why they are called watchmen (see what I did there).

Orient

"align or position (something) relative to the points of a compass or other specified positions." (Dictionary.com – Orient (verb) 1.)

Once we have observed a trigger, we now have a stimulus; something which has sparked our senses, fired up the Spirit, and which gets the blood pumping and mental synapses going. Now that a stimulus has occurred, we must then orient ourselves toward the event, cause, or person which has caught our attention or provoked our reaction and response.

This part of the process means that we do not turn away from what lies before us or that is come against us, but that we face it and bring it squarely into our focus.

The focus of our attention upon that which we have observed and aligning ourselves with it accepting that it has occurred or is occurring...this is how we orient ourselves and move into this part of the process.

Denial is a roadblock to this part of the process. Many people see things, hear things or find things out and their first response is to deny that it is possible or real. The very first thing I was taught when we came to this step is something every Impact Warrior MUST hear and understand.... **Never deny something is real or possible because it's the impossible and hard to believe that make the best weapons and that win wars!**

This step is not about validation...it is about orienting your focus and resources toward whatever has been observed. This does not mean we become single minded, not at all. The true skill here is being able to orient toward an observed stimulus while remaining observant to any other stimulus.

This is perhaps the greatest lesson of orientation. I was taught that to observe and then just try to keep it in mind while you begin scanning the horizon again leaves you vulnerable. The moment you go back to where you remembered the observation, it has moved, and you have lost it. I was always taught to orient my body in such a way as to keep what I observed in my peripheral while I continued observing. This is what orient means in this process. Moving and shifting our position to take in more fully what has been observed while remaining observant for any other event, cause, or stimulus.

Decide

We have now reached a pivotal part of the process where our thought and cognitive skills must weigh what we have observed, and what we have now oriented ourselves to. This is the part of the process where we now may begin to validate what we perceived.

We allow ourselves, now that we have oriented appropriately, to begin analysis of what we see, hear, touch, taste and smell. We begin to devise a plan and response based on its action, its threat, based against what we know is true, and against the armor or gear we have with us. This is where the Armor of God comes into play, where the Holy Spirit joins this process, and where our character must join with both to formulate the measured response required and appropriate.

In military training we develop intense muscle memory and skillset which is second nature to the individual. This is critical to this stage in the OODA loop process. When we see, feel, or hear a threat, we begin immediately to run through our gear and training mentally evaluating what is adequate to our response. We remember what we represent and stand for, and this all is thrown against our personal ethos and morals. From this we can go into the next step of the process, and without any of the previously stated being compromised.

For the Christian Impact Warrior this part in the process is where they stand in their armor fully, relying on it and the Holy Spirit to guide and empower them. They will measure the assessment of the observed stimulus based on their orientation and from them will flow the response which God desires as it is directed through His ways, means, and power.

If we adequately come to this process and remain in Christ, in the Spirit, and in the Armor of God then the decision will come from a Godly place and provide a Godly response. If we come to this part in the process with our own emotions, our own power, and our own heart...then we will see a very inappropriate response.

No warrior would come to this step and turn their back on their convictions, throw down all of their equipment and gear for a stick on the ground, choose to ignore all of their training, and rush naked and alone toward a well-armed enemy thinking what will happen next will be a positive outcome. But this is what we as Christians do when we choose to abandon God and all He has given us to respond from this step on our own and with weapons we have fashioned.

Decision must be based on what we have and are given along with what we know as true. The more you spend time in scripture with God, in prayer with God, bearing His Armor, the easier this step becomes to progress through. Until you have that deep and real relationship with God, you will find that this step is the one where the most time is spent to ensure proper flow into the next one. But once that relationship runs deep and real...this step will be the easiest as God's decision will flow with less and less interference from you.

Act

"For it is God which worketh in you both to will and to do of his good pleasure." (Philippians 2:13)

So now we come to the last part of this process... and that is how to act based on what we observed, how we have oriented toward it, and what our decision process has determined is appropriate. This part of the process is the verb portion of our reaction and response. It is the what, of what we have decided to respond with.

For most individuals this step can be lengthy as well. We have decided... but we delay action or draw it out for whatever reasons fear, emotion, or doubt may bring into this step. For the Warrior this is less of an issue because as we have shown they have intensity, and their alacrity does not allow for delay of very much.

The only other thing to state about action is that it is part of the process and it can also become the trigger for the loop to begin again. And this is important because that means we must observe our action and response, not just let it fly and go as if in auto pilot and on to the next mission.

Rinse & Repeat

Now that one action has concluded we must wash the past parts of the process away and repeat it again.

It is important that we do not carry over observations, orientation and decision simply because something is similar, the same, or a continuation. We must bring the previous parts with us now as part of the process, but only as historical and to be mixed in with the rest of our knowledge, wisdom, and God's leading.

This process repeats indefinitely and the more one uses it the faster and more efficient we become at it. But each loop must begin fresh and completely separate or we may find ourselves applying an outdated decision or miss any new information we would discover and be able to add into the process for a more refined and appropriate response (this is what we call growth).

*General information in opening paragraphs taken from: https://en.wikipedia.org/wiki/OODA_loop

Perspective

When we talk about reaction and response, we must also speak about one other principle if we truly want to master this process and have the controlled and measured response God requires of us. This is PERSPECTIVE.

There is a very great illustration of what I am trying to convey in 2 Kings chapter 6:

"And when the servant of the man of God was risen early, and gone forth, behold, an host compassed the city both with horses and chariots. And his servant said unto him, Alas, my master! how shall we do? 16And he answered, Fear not: for they that be with us are more than they that be with them. 17And Elisha prayed, and said, LORD, I pray thee, open his eyes, that he may see. And the LORD opened the eyes of the young man; and he saw: and, behold, the mountain was full of horses and chariots of fire round about Elisha. 18And when they came down to him, Elisha prayed unto the LORD, and said, Smite this people, I pray thee, with blindness. And he smote them with blindness according to the word of Elisha." (2 Kings 6:15-18)

What is the difference between Elisha's reaction and response, and that of his servant? *Perspective.*

I am positive that many of us would have reacted just as Elisha's servant did. If we woke up and went to get some water from the fridge, looked out of our kitchen window, and saw our house surrounded by a tactical SWAT team complete with armored vehicles ready to launch an assault against us...undoubtedly, most would freak out and the first things my kids would yell would be "DAD"!

But God desires us to have His perspective on what we observe, orient, decide and act toward. He desires that we have truly opened eyes and we see Him and all His glory when we react and respond. A deep relationship with God will give this to us. The deeper we are into a real heart, mind, and soul relationship with our creator and savior the more assuredly we will have the reaction and response of Elisha... **for we will have God's perspective on every matter, and that is all that truly matters in every reaction and response!**

The Impact Warrior in Impact Warfare

This first part of the book was about introducing the reader to the reality that our world and the lives we live exist in a state of real and active warfare. But that into this battlefield environment God has equipped us and called us out to be His impact upon this world, upon the lives of those around us, and upon this warfare.

Miracles and the supernatural are not fairy tales, and the power of the Holy Spirit is not only still alive and working...He is working in us and through us. All of the power and gifts of the Spirit are alive today and working today as they have never worked before.

What we read about and have heard about the power and gifts of days long past was just the beginning of what God is going to do in these last days...and yes, we are entering the end-times my friend.

God has called each and every one of you to be an Impact Warrior in Impact Warfare. What does this mean? It means that the first part of this book has been talking about you, it has been emboldening and encouraging you. You are a warrior of impact and your life, set in the Holy Spirit and in the calling of God, is the most impactful weapon and gift to this war-torn world imaginable.

You have the power to move mountains, you have the power of Paul to speak and to preach, you have the power of Elijah to call down fire from heaven if God is so inclined, and you have the power like Peter to walk on water. You were called to heal, to tread on scorpions and serpents, to raise the dead and to have dominion over the demonic and dark.

You were never called to sit and to watch from the sidelines, you were called to go forward and to be salt and light to a world shrouded in darkness and which has lost its savor. You were not meant to have a feckless and overwhelmed life; you were called to overcome in life and to have an efficacious life!

You are the one who is called to have the indwelling of the Holy Spirit. You are called because you have the two core character traits we discussed. You were called because the catalysts of character exist in you in a predetermined formula that makes up your individual mission and ministry. You were called to take up the whole Armor of God. You were called because your reaction and response is the answer of God to this broken and evil world.

You were called because you are an Impact Warrior and you are meant to impact this warfare!

You may be saying right now that this cannot be you, that you do not have these things in you right now, that your past is too much to overcome, that you are not ready for something like this, or that you have too much to get through before you could ever be used of God.

Well, I have heard this stated many times over the years and it cannot be attributed directly to any one person, but it speaks to your reservations...

"God does not call the already equipped and well qualified, He equips and qualifies those He calls". (1 Corinthians 1:27,28)

What is going on around us is taking place whether you accept it, ignore it, or choose to deny it. You can choose to sit back, stand by, and be a victim of it...or you can sit up, stand up, and claim victory over it!

This book began where we all must, with explaining a little about who God desires to be in you, it introduces us to ourselves, and it details the equipment and expectations we have been given. This is by no means an exhaustive or comprehensive compendium on the subject. It is designed to be your introduction, your motivation, your encouragement, whatever it is that you need right now. For some it is to begin, for others it is to inspire. For many it will fan a cooling flame, for some it is to trim the wick and keep the light shining bright.

Whatever the first part of this book has been for you, it is just part one. You must not stop reading yet as we are about to enter into a subject that is critical to your life and to your impact in this warfare.

We are about to enter the word and world of prayer. We are about to find the powder behind every ignition and the direct line to God Himself.

Let's continue to go forward in this world for Jesus with MAXIMUM IMPACT!

PART II: Impact Prayer

Do you know what prayer is? I mean really…has anyone ever explained it to you? Have you ever deeply studied scripture to find out what it is? Do you know that this is the most powerful revelation that God desires in His children for them to use in warfare and in knowing Him?

Sure, we say our bedtime prayers, we bow our heads with everyone else in church or at gatherings, we say our grace before meals, and we make sure to interject the expected "I will pray for you" or "I will keep you in prayer" when we finish conversations with others on the trials and trivialities of our days and lives. But we must ask ourselves, is this the fullness of what God asks and desires of us in prayer? Is this what prayer is meant to be, or is it meant to be more?

Prayer is the most integral part of our warfare in the spiritual and in living the fullness of life in the physical with God each moment and with every breath.

IMPACT PRAYER is prayer in the Holy Spirit that is not only wielded in combat as our greatest and most intrusive and effective of weapons, it is also the unrestricted and uninterrupted direct line between ourselves and the almighty Living God!

Impact Prayer is not some tool for success or formula to get what we want in life, it is the vehicle whereby God's desire for our life and the lives of others becomes manifest and brought to bear in this world. It is what divides the darkness and brings healing to the broken and diseased as well as breaking chains which bind and strongholds which lay siege to our minds.

In part two of this book we will shine the light on true prayer, on effective prayer, on Impact Prayer. We will dispel the myths and poor teachings from over the years and bring back the old ways of direct, manifest, and dynamic prayer which empowers the church and dethrones evil where it dares to sit and come against the light.

Let's learn to kneel before God so that we may stand before all men and all the spiritual forces we face!

Communication Equals Intelligence

"Then shall ye call upon me, and ye shall go and pray unto me, and I will hearken unto you. And ye shall seek me, and find me, when ye shall search for me with all your heart. And I will be found of you, saith the LORD" (Jeremiah 29:11-14)

God desires to hear from you. You would be hard pressed to find a loving father here on earth who does not desire to hear from his children and to share in a conversation to find out all that has happened, what things are they interested in now, what areas might need some counsel or assistance, and just to hear their voice as it warms the heart and spirit.

This is even more true of our Heavenly Father. You may say not so, as God already knows everything and does not need this information like an earthly father would... well,

101

as a father of four myself I can tell you that is false. There are many times when I already know about something one of my sons or daughters has done or had happen in their life. I may have been given the heads up and the details but I still long for when I get to hear it from my child directly. There is just a simple yet very real joy when your child comes to you and shares their life and takes the time to ask about yours.

This is part of "relationship". The same can be said between best friends, spouses, and other loved ones as with my example above for a father and child. There is just something overwhelmingly powerful about the connections we make when we are open and sharing between us. The trust is developed, the empathy enlarged, the whole dynamic between the two just explodes in how it becomes anticipated and just a part of what makes each person whole.

This is first-and-foremost the design of prayer since the fall in the garden. Before the fall, Adam spoke with God face-to-face as they walked together in the cool of the day. And even though God has spoken to mankind directly numerous times since then…it has become prayer which is our primary form of communication and relationship with God. Prayer is how we share with our Father.

Taking the Time to Pray

I wanted to begin by making this point on prayer and truly stressing its communication and relationship aspects before ever getting into its uses in warfare and for the Impact Warrior in their everyday battles.

Prayer is absolute in its raw, dynamic, forceful and vehement power but is not just for combat and battle. Yes, it is part of the Armor of God and a most effective weapon...but only to those who know how it functions and works outside of warfare and in relationship.

To call upon a power one does not truly know is magik and strictly forbidden by scripture. It is also the surest way to be in contact with the wrong power pretending to be, and have, everything you desire. True prayer, on the other hand, is a call upon the deep supernatural in a way of directed communication with a known power...and for the Impact Warrior and Christian that is the Holy Spirit and nothing less than God Almighty. You must KNOW and have a REAL personal relationship with God to be able to communicate in that relationship with Him. Again, to not know Him means there can be no true communication. This is evident in John 9:31 where it states *"Now we know that God heareth not sinners: but if any man be a worshipper of God, and doeth his will, him he heareth"*.

We MUST know Jesus Christ, we MUST know the Holy Spirit, we MUST know the Father. We must know to whom we pray and to what purpose prayer serves. We need to know that prayer is not a form of vending machine in that we deposit a little work or time and then ask for a specific need just expecting it to fall down in the same way we get G7 when we enter the correct change at the snack machine (don't laugh, there are many "Christians" who treat God and prayer in this manner due to false teaching).

Taking the time to pray is not about building up brownie points that we can call in later. Taking the time to pray is about developing and nurturing a relationship where we eventually understand that God knows what we need before we even ask (Matthew 6:8) and that even if we do not know what to ask, He assists us by His Spirit (Romans 8:26-27). So, knowing this in our heart we come to the knowledge that prayer is about conversation, communication, and communion with our Abba Father and that in this full engaging fellowship and intimacy an exchange takes place of more than just need...and therein every possible need is satiated.

This is why we must know God and take the time to pray...so that we understand it is the depth of our communion that comes from communication, which is at its core our heart and spirit in conversation.

Saying all of this I want to reiterate how absolutely important it is to work on your personal relationship with God and to develop that loving and lasting walk with Him. Learn to stop in moments and share them, learn to set yourself apart to give to Him without distraction and interruption. Take the time to show God how important and integral He is to you and what you will see returned to you will change your life!

When you take the time to pray, God will fill that time with all of Himself. God will reveal to you all that He has planned, all that He knows you need, and supply all that He knows is necessary for you to stand in Him.

Intelligence for Battle

"Surely the Lord GOD will do nothing, but he revealeth his secret unto his servants the prophets." (Amos 3:7)

Now we return to prayer as it is understood in warfare. As I have shown, prayer opens up a channel between you and God...it develops a deep and real relationship. A relationship to where you seek God's counsel and wisdom, and where He shares his intelligence and plans.

Every modern-day soldier will tell you that communication is critical to being able to operate in battle. Your main communication keeps you up to date on positioning, intelligence, and coordinates your moves with the overall move of the whole. Communication equals intelligence, and this is even more so when we speak of communication through prayer.

The spiritual realm which we battle against has an intricate intelligence network and works with millennia of experience in this combat. They know and understand the laws of the universe and work in a power not only beyond our grasp, but that is mostly unseen.

When a warrior comes against an enemy with far superior firepower and capabilities, they rely on intelligence and on being guided through whatever plan will allow them to overcome and achieve the desired outcome of the one who has sent them. We are sent by God, and God's desired outcome is achieved when we allow Him to guide our steps and to bring to bear His power against the darkness we face and against all of the plans of evil in this warfare.

Prayer brings us before the throne of the Almighty and opens us to hear His word and to align with the Holy Spirit. This alignment will reveal the plans and deceit of the enemy and guide us in what is truly occurring in realms we cannot see and in the minds of those pawns that Satan is using in his schemes. We see this when God revealed to Jeremiah what was being plotted against him *"And the LORD hath given me knowledge of it, and I know it: then thou shewedst me their doings. But I was like a lamb or an ox that is brought to the slaughter; and I knew not that they had devised devices against me"*. (Jeremiah 11:18)

Imagine knowing what the enemy has planned, what their next moves will be, and even better… what their motives are in why attacks are coming against you. This intelligence allows one to be prepared and to work with the Holy Spirit, who has shown us all of this, and to fight with the upper hand literally in every situation which the devil is trying to use to place us outside of God and to bend this world to his hand in this war.

But there is even more to our communication and prayer with God and where it brings us in our battles.

Evil for Good

"Fear not: for am I in the place of God? But as for you, ye thought evil against me; but God meant it unto good, to bring to pass, as it is this day" (Genesis 50:20)

"And we know that all things work together for good to them that love God, to them who are the called according to his purpose." (Romans 8:28)

Prayer is primarily about building that relationship with God and bringing us into His intelligence and into His place of knowledge for battle. This allows us to stand in His Armor and to be overcomers. This brings us to a place where we have foreknowledge and the running ability of having the optimal intelligence and orders which find us part of a coordinated plan of our Father in His victory.

There is also another benefit to our communication with God and the deep relationship it builds. This relationship brings us to a place where everything we go through, everything that comes against us, no matter the good or the bad...God now is working it all for His purpose and all things begin to work together for good.

We are imperfect and very weak servants. This can be seen by reading the lives of even those who have come face-to-face with God, for they too have failed at times. We all fall short and we all have a past. The good news is that God knows all of this and will use all of this to His good and to His ultimate plan for this world. In prayer we know this because He reveals it to us. It was a life of prayer and faith that allowed Joseph to know that through it all, God had a plan. And as he continued to seek God and to be in His plan, he came to the place of truly understanding this principle as he relayed to his brothers the forgiveness he had within and that the past they shared is what led to the present in which they now shared God's blessings. God never forsakes us, always forgives us, and always works for us if we are in Him!

I hope that it is now becoming a clear picture as to what prayer should start as in us and that I have provided a guide into where we begin and to where it can develop and go. When you engage prayer, make it always about engaging God your Father and all else as secondary to the privilege and moment of connecting with your God. If you know nothing else about prayer but this you will have more than you need and all else will fall into place naturally as He leads you deeper into Himself.

There is of course more to prayer, and much to understand when it comes to utilizing prayer in the battle we are called to. As we move into the next chapter to discuss the basics of prayer and then further in this book into application and development, remember this chapter and always fall back to the perfect design and purpose of our prayer...time with your Abba, Father.

What Then Is Prayer?

"I exhort therefore, that, first of all, supplications, prayers, intercessions, and giving of thanks, be made for all men" (1 Timothy 2:1)

No matter where I go, or to what kind of group I find myself teaching or fellowshipping with, the question of "how then shall we pray" or "what exactly is prayer" is always asked by someone in one manner or another. Many people are afraid to ask this question out loud for fear of embarrassment that they do not know, so often I am pulled aside in private. The truth is we need to speak up. More people in the church than we would think are asking this question and need to know what prayer is.

For many, prayer is just how we get what we need and want, it is a set formulaic recitation of words and scripture to affect the blessings of God upon our lives. It is ritual and tradition which we move through based on what we see others do. Or worse yet, we rely on others we think more adept to guide us in prayer as we feel God delights in fancy oration or skilled prose.

This is not prayer which brings down fire from the heavens…this is not prayer that effects and affects the world and those living within it…this is not prayer that brings healing and wholeness…this is not prayer which forces back the powers of darkness and which wages war against their strongholds and possessions.

What prayer like that has become is ineffectual, and it is leaving too many feeling God does not hear them or that they somehow are not as connected as others. We have lost power to press against the world and against evil…but the failure here hits hardest in that too many are lacking the real, deep, and personal relationship with God that prayer feeds and strengthens.

Impact Warriors MUST have a very penetrating prayer life. It is not recommended, it is required. As we have discussed in part one of this book…we are all called to be warriors in Christ, to have impact, and that we are part of this warfare whether we choose to be or not.

Prayer cannot be placed into "when available" openings on a calendar or schedule. Prayer cannot just be the simple, nominal interactions with God that we are prescribed to perform as expected because we are "Christians". How we manage prayer and envelop ourselves in prayer speaks to how

God lives in us. We must begin by knowing prayer and understanding prayer.

The verse above from 1 Timothy is unique in that it utilizes all four Greek words we translate and understand as prayer in the New Testament. These four terms also tell us a lot about the makeup of what prayer is and has as its intention.

Each term used by Paul can be personal or corporate, and it can also be selfish or selfless.

The Four Main Applications of Prayer

Personal & Corporate

"Personal" means that it is applied to our person as well as something we individually make use of, while "corporate" simply means it is in congress with someone else or with numerous others. People make a great deal of noise about the difference between the two...but it is quite simply the difference between praying as one in the Spirit for a cause or outcome and praying with others in the Spirit in agreement for a like cause and outcome.

One thing to remember as well is that personal prayer does not mean alone. When we pray in the Spirit and live with the Holy Spirit indwelling, we are never alone. There are those who seek corporate prayer alone because they do not like to pray alone or simply do not feel comfortable at it. This is not prayer or a relationship.

An illustration that really brings this to light is when we really think of our relationship with God as a relationship.

What would you say to someone if you were in a relationship and they only spoke to you when you were in a group or gathering together? Whenever you are alone, they will only speak to you if they are in desperate need or danger, and then it is only directed at you, not a conversation with you. Would you say your relationship was healthy and strong? Would you even say you were really in a relationship with that other person at all? Does that hit home?

Personal and corporate prayer are required for healthy prayer and relationship. Make sure we know and understand this. Our relationship requires personal time and attention, but it must also go out and be joined with others as this is the definition of Church and fellowship.

Selfish & Selfless

"Selfish" means that it is applied to the self as well as something we individually need or can make use of, while "selfless" simply means it is for others or with someone or something else's need to be met. These terms can be extrapolated as well into numerous teachings but quite simply prayer directed at ourselves is selfish and toward others is selfless.

You hear many teachers telling their audience that selfless prayer is the prayer God desires, as it is devoid of selfish desire and it is us applying God and bringing God to bear for others, which they say is the "Golden rule" and/or some altruistic way in which we receive what we need by placing others before our self. I differ on this point and let me explain why this oversimplifies the meaning of selfish and turns people away from bringing their direct needs before God as they desire not to be selfish in prayer or in their relationship.

Now, the term selfish may seem negative. And most times when we speak of mankind selfishness is negative. But in prayer there will always be times of selfish prayer as we have needs, and we have questions, and we have desires, all which we would like to bring God into. Yes, it can be altruistic to place others before our self, but it is naïve to think God does not wish to hear and know what we require and desire as well.

The difference in true Spirit-filled prayer is that the selfish prayers we have are to gain more of God in our selves. We are asking for Him to come in and to be in us. We desire healing and release from pain not just because we hurt, but because this disease, pain or disorder keeps us from being fully given unto Him. It distracts, disables, or in some other way detracts from what would be a place God is currently involved.

Selfish and selfless can both be used negatively or positively and both are needed in healthy prayer. To only focus on one and not the other is incomplete conversation and relationship. Just remember it is in relationship and this will keep you from the negative of both, for the negative of both is in taking and giving without God or His desire and heart.

The Four Main Types of Prayer

The important thing to remember as we discuss the four main types of prayer in scripture, and as we have expressed in Timothy, is that the four types of prayer are all prayer. None is greater or lesser simply by their type as each applied in the Spirit is powerful to its purpose.

These four types become expressed in numerous ways in the Bible. There are many sub-types and expressions of each type. For this book and for its purpose it is important to understand the four main types and then to let the Spirit take each and use it to whatever purpose is desired of God. It is these purposes which lend to the longer lists of types we see everywhere. For the Impact Warrior it is crucial we know the foundation of the main four and then through experience and study we see them bloom into the various expressions that are the colors God paints with, in and through prayer.

Deeseis - Supplication

Deeseis (deh'-ay-sis) is defined by Strong's (1162) as "a need, entreaty" and is known primarily in the Bible as a prayer of supplication. It gives the implication of a felt need that is personal and urgent. These are requests from men to their God. These are the type of prayers where we entreat God to hear us on behalf of an expressed need with urgency.

This type can be translated as a "petition" or even as a "supplication", both of which give us the picture of asking earnestly with intensity and as a pleading on our knees before one who has the ultimate power to provide the desired remedy.

When we implore God's aid in any particular matter at hand or at heart, we are engaged in *Deeseis* prayer. This type of prayer has real power in the Spirit setting fire to emotion, empathy, mercy, and all of those parts of us that desire God to hear our cause and case and to perform upon His character for resolution.

This type of prayer is also effective at surrendering our anxiety and fears to God. We are called to practice supplication not only to bring these things before almighty God...but also to remove them from our burden and in faith know that He has taken them.

Proseuché – General Prayer

Proseuché (pros-yoo-khay') is defined by Strong's (4335) as "an exchange" or "oratory towards" and is known primarily in the Bible as general prayer. It gives the implication of an exchange between two parties... a conversation if you will. These are the type of prayers where we speak to God and converse with Him. These prayers don't require a reaction or any action from God, or from ourselves. All they require is the desire to converse.

When I think of this type of prayer I always get a picture of those times when I am walking in the woods and engaging God in conversation to inform Him, seek Him, and to open myself up before Him in the most unprotected and unguarded fashion. This is a powerful type of prayer, for it builds not for need, worship, or for God's action. It can have any of those facets, but at its core this is prayer of building relationship. This is us getting to know God and letting Him hear, expressed by us, what He already knows but longs to hear from us.

An interesting point to elaborate on this word is that is can also be used of a place, or house, that is devoted to God.

A house of prayer. A place which is marked by its devotion and devotedness to that key function. The key is in the word devoted and this is what makes this style of prayer unique from others. It is defined by devotion.

This is why this particular term is used for prayer when Jesus states in Matthew 17:21 that those kinds of demons only go out by "prayer and fasting". Fasting coupled with Devotion toward God in exchange with Him leads to His power manifesting with such strength that even the toughest demons will flee!

Enteuxis – Intercession

Enteuxis (ent'-yook-sis) is defined by Strong's (1783) as an "intersection which literally 'hits the mark'" and is known primarily in the Bible as intercession. It gives the implication of finding the mark to hit and asking God to hit it on behalf of another.

This is warfare prayer which is brought before the throne of God on another's behalf and so that they may be used by God or that God may use you to affect the outcome necessary and needed for another. This is directed intervention sought by us from God for those who either cannot seek it for themselves, will not seek it for themselves, or do not have the relationship with God to know to seek it for themselves, or for their cause.

Intercession is powerful, extremely powerful, as it calls down the armament and artillery of God upon the spiritual which is wreaking havoc and darkness in the physical. We are asking God to attack territory we do not stand in and cannot stand in. This is God's Will coming to the aid of those whose free will does not or will not reach out to Him directly.

We will learn a lot more about Intercession as we delve into the chapter dedicated to discussing this weapon and use of *enteuxix* prayer. We will find that this is not only a type of prayer, but a use of prayer in combat with the spiritual enemy we stand against.

Eucharistia – Thanksgiving

Eucharistia (yoo-khar-is-tee'-ah) is defined by Strong's (2169) as "the giving of thanks, gratitude, and thankfulness" and is known primarily in the Bible as thanksgiving. It gives the implication of worship and the pouring out of our gratitude to a merciful and gracious God.

You may recognize a key to something much greater in the Greek pronunciation of this type. It is pronounced the same as eucharist because we get the word *eucharist* from the Greek *eucharistia*. This is an important note as the term eucharist has the meaning of oblation and communion, as does the original Greek term. Oblation is the act of giving an offering and communion is sharing and participation.

These prayers are a sacrifice to God and us giving to Him the glory, praise, and charged gratitude we have for Him and for all He is and does. This sacrifice is often shared with others as we worship and as we share our testimony in thanks to the Loving God who saves. While these prayers, like all of them, can be personal...this prayer is by far the most corporate of them all in how it is used and in how it breaks out when people are gathered together in worship and prayer to God.

Worship of this nature is often sung or placed in poetic speech as we search for the words and proper vehicle to elevate our prayer and to express what is burning inside of us. This type of prayer is electric and electrifying and often has the effect corporately and personally of rapture and of ignition of the Spirit within.

Intimacy

Where we have focused so much on intensity in part one of this book, we must couple it here with a term of like nature but that speaks to the side of prayer and relationship that the Impact Warrior seeks and stands in. Intimacy is an intense word and one which draws an emotional and mental response and reaction from everyone in some way. Intimacy is where many find discomfort. That discomfort is where God wishes to meet you and to begin His work in you.

God loves to work where we are outside of our comfort. He loves to call us out of the comfortable and into the compatible with Him. Intimacy is this place in our relationship with God and intimacy is where all real prayer lives and surges from. Intimacy carries with it such powerful terms as familiarity, affection, and love. This is why and where we get that God is love...because God is in the intimacy and intimacy is a place of familial affection which is stronger than any other bond in the physical and/or spiritual.

We must train ourselves to live in intimacy with intensity, for as Impact Warriors intensity is how we do things right? We must enter here with no fear or discomfort. We must enter initially outside of our comfort zone so that we are comfortable no longer any other place than in this place with God.

Confidence and communion with God are built here as we become more and more enthralled with God the Father, God the Son, and God the Holy Spirit.

Warrior Prayer

We have looked into the what and why of prayer and this is the first step in the warrior knowing intimately what prayer is, and why it is necessary. When we think of warriors, we think of brutish, muscle-bound, armor clad, strong men and women. But this is not how God sees a warrior. God sees a warrior in all those who allow Him to work in them and through them. To be used for war makes one a warrior in God's eyes...just ask Gideon.

So, when we speak of prayer, and the types of prayer, and the applications of prayer, are there different kinds of prayer? The answer is yes. In this world we see ineffectual prayer, unanswered prayer, misdirected prayer, and often the performance of prayer. But these kinds of prayer are direct opposition to true prayer, warrior prayer. When an Impact Warrior wields prayer, it is as a part of the Armor of God and as a weapon. Prayer is not used without intention, without expectation, without direction, and never as a performance as warfare is not the stage, it is the battlefield.

Basic training in the military is just that, to train one in the basics of their intended service and expectations. What this chapter has been is equivalent to basic training on prayer. Knowing the what and why of pray is just an opening into the how, when, and where of prayer and its use.

As we go into the next three chapters that is what I will seek to do. I will set out to give you a fuller picture of prayer in warfare. With each of the next three chapters I have focused on a particular usage of prayer so that we may see how it is used, where it is useful, and when we should reach for that particular type and application when the battle rages around us and the road gets tough. My desire is for you to know prayer in such a way that it is natural and available to you for its purpose and so that you can go deep in your relationship with God. For it is only in the depth of God's love and Spirit that we truly begin to operate at the real impact levels He desires.

I want to end this chapter by coming back to the topic of what prayer is and is not. Prayer is not weakness, it never was. To the enemy both physical and spiritual it looks like weakness when we drop to our knees and we surrender to God. If we saw a soldier on the battlefield drop to their knees, we would see this as exhaustion, weakness, or even perhaps as their dying moments. But when you see that soldier catch their breath, stand up swiftly and with determination, you know that the battle is back on and their resolve will be a determining factor in the next few moments of combat.

Prayer is what we seek in those moments. When we drop to our knees, lift up our hands, lower our heads, it is not for any other outcome than for God to come in, for God to bring the fire, and when He does, we too stand up filled with resolve and determination...and with the Holy Spirit on fire within! And the next few moments will bring forth the miraculous and will decide the outcome by His hand and to His conclusion. That breath we catch when we fall to His feet is the breath of God that is filled and fueled with the Fire of God straight from His presence and ready to ignite the powder behind the explosive nature of the Impact Warrior in possession of Impact Prayer.

We ourselves become the atomic weapon which changes the tide of the warfare around us and which drives back the enemy from even the most fierce and well laid strongholds and fortifications. When we are in prayer, they do not have a prayer...pun intended.

Keep this in mind as we read ahead and continue to develop our intimacy and intensity with this weapon and communication device that God has granted us. For our prayer goes straight to the throne room of the king and rises before the King of Kings Himself as He stands ready and in the place of intensity and intimacy to which he has called us to Himself.

IMPACT WARFARE

The Prayer of Faith and Fervency

"The effectual fervent prayer of a righteous man availeth much." (James 5:16)

So, we have the deep and real personal relationship that prayer can breed in us, and the knowledge of what prayer is and can be for us. Now, we must set fire to our prayer life and how we wield it in life and battle. We must let our prayer become nothing less than Spirit-led, faith-filled, passionate, intense, raw, electric, alive, all encompassing, fervent prayer.

We cannot stand now in this knowledge and relationship and simply mouth feckless words which listlessly fall on fruitless ground. We must stand with words that come from an ignited heart and which bear such magnitude that they never fall to the ground, but which shake the very earth to bring forth the fruits of God's desire and Spirit.

That last sentence is key… our prayer must shake the ground that darkness seeks to take, it must liquify the dust upon which evil stands. It must bring such force to bear that what is brought to battle is the fiery presence of the Living God Himself in answer to the cries and petitions of His obedient and expectant children.

Prayer can be the surgical arrow of our directed seeking of God's Will into a particular situation or upon a needed circumstance. Prayer can also be the nuclear atomic blast of the supernatural brought against everything spiritual and physical that dares to come against it or set itself up opposed to it.

Prayer was never meant to have no effect; no, it was meant to affect life and creation in the most ardent of ways. If you pray and see nothing happen, then you are not wielding prayer in the Spirit and your relationship with God may be where your focus is needed most. Even if God does not choose to answer your prayer, you should feel the palpable force of the Holy Spirit moving about you, and within you. Unanswered prayer always has an "answer", we must simply be open to seeing what God is doing within and around our request.

This is an important thing to note…prayer is not just auditory and/or some feeling we get. Prayer has visual and non-visual cues and intricacies just like communication we have in all relationships in our life. I have known my wife for almost twenty-five years and trust me, there are sometimes more non-verbal aspects to our conversations than verbal. This is relationship, and in relationship with God the same will become true the deeper you become invested and involved in communion with Him.

Knowing that there will be an answer is the formation and fundamental substance of the faith we are about to discuss, the faith which is key to prayer.

The Key of Faith

"Now faith is the substance of things hoped for, the evidence of things not seen." (Hebrews 11:1)

Faith is the inherent conviction in something we are committed to with all of our heart, mind and being. Faith does not rest in the "I am pretty sure He will answer" or in the "I don't see why God would not". No, faith rests in the whole-hearted knowledge that God WILL answer and that we will see His reply and response. This is the substance of our hope and the evidence for things not seen that we are told is the premise of faith.

Faith is the unwavering, solid and unshakeable compelling in our soul that God is…that God will do…and that God always fulfils His promises! Faith is unquestioning in its nature yet always questioning what we hear, see, and experience to find God there. It is a seeking part of us that knows without doubt that God is real, and which searches every moment for His presence.

I also defined faith in the earlier chapter on the Armor of God as active and evident. Faith has substance and is the power behind things seen and unseen. One's faith is the belief in the evident presence and reality of their hope…and for the Impact Warrior of God, that hope is Jesus Christ and the very promises of almighty God.

Just as a physical key enters a lock to turn and unlock its mechanisms so that it may be opened… So, the key of faith enters the mechanisms of our prayer to turn the situation before us, it unlocks and opens the doors of heaven. Our faith brings all of the character traits we discussed, catalysts and everything within the Impact Warrior into an impassioned wholehearted experience with God. That experience is intimacy in a way like no other moment that could ever be shared with another. It is an opening of the channel between you and God where His real, and powerful, presence and purpose flow into the supernatural and the natural. Prayer opens opportunity and manifests God's answer to anything and everything to which it is directed.

Do you believe this? Do you know with all of your being that God answers prayer? Do you have an unyielding sense of complete and absolute certainty in the promises of God and that He speaks into the line of communication that prayer opens between you and Him?

Answering yes to the above is faith…it is the active and all-encompassing surety that we have in the person of God. The prayer of faith is not a prayer of maybe something taking place, it is the place where something does. When you pray in faith you rise with assurance!

The devil knows that faith is power, and he knows the weakness which drains faith and dispels its effectiveness.

Doubt is the questioning of all that I have presented in this chapter so far. It is the antithesis to assurance, to surety, to knowing in our whole being that God will. In-fact it turns "God will", into "I sure hope He does". You must understand it is never about questioning God, it is about questioning ourselves and the core of our relationship and trust that we have in God.

Building Our Faith

The way we build on our faith, and the way in which it becomes bullet-proof to all that darkness throws at it, is in our keeping observant with our eyes wide open to all that moves and takes place about us. Never taking our eyes off of Jesus for even a second, and watching with anticipation for Him to move in, around, and through what is in the space around us builds up our faith.

Faith is exercised. It grows and expands as it is put out and placed into the atmosphere of our belief. If you hold it too tight it will never reach exponential levels which can only be defined as impactful. This is why God calls us to step out in faith (see 2 Corinthians 5:7 & Hebrews 11:8). He knows that faith is expanded when we create an expanse for Him to occupy. By enlarging the area in which we walk and step out in faith we have allowed ourselves to experience faith in action and this leads to an increased understanding of faith and in its workings.

The best way to increase in faith, and therein increase your prayerful impact, is to use it! Get out there and put it into practice and seek God's Will and His desire. Then attach your petition and your prayer to it with everything you have…that is what we will discuss next.

The Passion of Fervency

"fervent in spirit; serving the Lord; Rejoicing in hope; patient in tribulation; continuing instant in prayer" (Romans 12:11-12)

We have spoken of intensity before in part one of this book. Intensity, passion, fire, and overall investment and motivation that make up the character and catalysts of a warrior in Christ and who is set for impact in battle with the supernatural and natural forces against us. We have shown how this investment and passion must be directed and how that intensity with direction of the Holy Spirit can affect and have effect on this world in absolutely atomic and explosive ways. This is the heartfelt definition of fervent.

When scripture tells us to be fervent in service, fervent in prayer, and to fervently long for something, it is asking us to have a burning hot soul-level feeling of excitement and anticipation to see something come to fruition. This is not simply some "passion" of ours as many people relate as the meaning of fervent…no it is a fire-in-the-bones comprehensive need and desire to see God move!

This is what God is calling us to in prayer. That when we are in the Spirit, we are in the fire of that Spirit and letting it drive us not into a frenzy, but into fervency.

To a warrior in prayer, fervency is seen in that you do not go into prayer when the calendar on your phone reminds you that your scheduled prayer time has come. No, it is when you check your phone every ten minutes because you cannot wait until your scheduled time to pray gets here. Or better still, you look and just cannot wait so you dive into your prayer time early because to wait even a minute longer to be in communion with your Father in heaven consumes your every thought.

This does not mean that we forsake our daily duties and responsibilities. We are not called to be constantly checking our watches as if we are hourly employees just waiting to pounce out the door when the clock strikes five o'clock. What this means is that we have time set aside for God, we know when moments call for prayer, and we must then fight the urge to get before Him without delay, so much so that it is like fighting breathing. Prayer has become a biological and integral function to our existence.

That sounds pretty out there…but that is what prayer must become for us. It cannot be something we forget to do or rush through because we have somewhere else to be. Prayer must be so habitual that to stop would be as hard as any smoker or drug user's withdrawal would be. Our physical being would become sick without it.

Seeing it through

Fervency is also that drive which brings us to a place where we see things through. To be fervent in prayer is to be meaningful and to be diligent in your purpose for prayer.

One who is fervent in prayer is someone who sees it through to the completion of their petition. Many of the great intercessory prayer warriors come to mind and the way in which they bring things before God and they kneel for hours, days, weeks and sometimes years to see it through. That is determination and that is faith in practice. That is placing your full intention upon the needs of others and the desire of God to see things through and to see His victory and glory in the fulfilment of prayer.

Another wonderful illustration of fervent prayer is the prayer of a mother for one of her children. I have heard such marvelous stories of mothers who never stopped praying with tears and their whole heart for one of their lost children to find Jesus and to hear the call of God upon their heart. One mother told me that she spent thirty years in prayer, praying every day for her son who was addicted to drugs and who had been in and out of rehab over thirteen times. She said there were many times when she thought he had hit bottom and would listen to the Gospel and feel the conviction…but each time he would fall deeper into addiction, depression and despair. Finally, she said after a failed suicide attempt her son was laying in the hospital and out of nowhere asked to speak to a chaplain. That simple request from the grip of despair would lead to him accepting Christ as his savior and turning his whole life over to God. The last I had heard he was leading youth interventions with a ministry that reaches out to homeless and abused children.

Thirty years is a very long time to stay faithful, to stay fervent in prayer, and to see God move. But to an Impact Warrior who is filled with the Holy Spirit, who wears the whole Armor of God, who is faithful, and fervent in prayer…thirty years, even 120 years are well spent in the pursuit of God's desire and to see Him move. Moses is a perfect picture of this, and we are called to be as well.

Under Attack

Prayer is so critical and imperative to our walk with God that if you answer His call and you step into the warrior life, Satan will come at you with every scheme and arrow in his arsenal. You will live a life under attack, and if there is one area that Satan will focus above any other it will be against your faith and fervency. Doubt will be his attack against your faith and the dry, cold, impassive places to which he will try to drag you will be his attack against your fervency.

We discussed the Armor of God and I hope that you understood the need and importance of bearing that armor and standing in it fully applied each moment and with every breath. Satan and the powers of darkness will not relent, they will not concede defeat, and they will never stop coming against you if you are in Christ. Understand this and know it.

Live with this always in your view and you will never take those distractions and detours that always seem to pull you away from prayer, away from fellowship, and away from those places of faith as loosely again. You will see them for what they are, and you will learn to fall into prayer and let God stand you up in even the most ferocious of storms. The more you develop and become locked into prayer you will find the battles becoming more intense, but the force of God against all that comes against you will come with intensity that even Satan could not imagine.

Make prayer natural, and part of your very biological existence and you will see the truly miraculous become the everyday expected. You will see the power and presence of God come into the atmosphere to bring healing, to bring deliverance, and to answer prayer in the face of the constant pressing of darkness.

Nothing shuts the mouth of evil faster than answered prayer and nothing brings fear into the dark more than an Impact Warrior resting in faith and fervent in prayer!

Prayer will have you in direct conflict and combat with all of the principalities, powers, rulers of darkness and spiritual wickedness in this world. Prayer will bring you into the warfare around us as a beacon of light which pierces even the most deep-seated, pitch black, shroud of rebellion that Satan can muster on this earth. We have shown the communication and intelligence that prayer brings us into, we have shown a basic outline of what prayer is, and we have shown that faith and fervency are what set impact prayer apart from the performance of prayer that we see so often today.

Prayer is indelibly linked to spiritual warfare by its very nature. In the next chapter we will bring prayer into the arena of spiritual warfare and take all that we have discussed and put forth and bring it to bear in battle. Being in deep relationship with our Father and having the faith and fervency of a life dedicated and immersed in prayer will now bring us into our arsenal and armory.

Let's now look into how explosive our prayer can be and how it can be directed to maximum impact and with the power to shake the supernatural and natural worlds.

Imprecation, Impartation and Intercession

"For the weapons of our warfare are not carnal, but mighty
through God to the pulling down of strong holds"
(2 Corinthians 10:4)

Prayer is something that exists. It has substance and it is alive with the flowing of the Spirit and the intention of its wording and directed course. Our prayers rise up before the throne of the Living God (Psalm 141:2) and they trample the forces of darkness that come against God's prayer warriors (Psalm 44:5).

Too often we think of prayer like we think of our daily chatter. We know our words can sting and bite, yet we think of them as just some vibration in the air, some wisp of a spoken word. While prayer has a spoken, and at times unspoken, element to it, those words are far from some simple vibration of air waves and abstract idea we send out for base communication. No, prayer is the reality of words which have weight from a density of Spirit in which they are sent and with the embodiment of the directed intention and intensity of forethought with which they were woven together to deliver their purpose married to the Will of the Almighty.

Where our everyday words can cause an emotional response and even take someone aback by their strength and forceful delivery, prayer can tear down the strongholds built around true emotion which hinder growth and healthy emotional response and living. Prayer can blast the supernatural from off their feet and knock the natural to their knees before the mighty, strong, and brilliant presence of God. Where our words can sweep others away like a wave, both for the positive and for the negative. Prayer comes with the full magnitude of the ocean behind it to pound against all that stands opposed to the Lord and delivers all that He declares, promised and decrees, to His good.

We have spent some time really driving home how powerful prayer is and why it is such a prime weapon in combat. Now we have come to a place where it is time to break down a few uses of prayer and the application of them in warfare. Prayer, in the hands of an Impact Warrior, in the hands of one who is surrendered to Jesus Christ, can bring judgement, can bring God's blessings, and can bring the cause of others to bear in ways which cannot be conceived of or even imagined. This is why prayer is truly miraculous and why it has such manifest power in the supernatural and the natural.

Here Comes the Boom

When you see a soldier carrying their weapon you can usually tell if they are new or seasoned. There is a walk and a way in which veterans and those with real life experience will stride when they are doing anything in life. That way of carrying themselves and their weapon is called comfort.

I can tell you with much experience myself, that the more you use and carry your weapons and handle them in combat of any kind, even if it is just years of heavy and consistent training, it all becomes second nature. You develop that respect for yourself and the weapon which will always have you carry it with confidence and comfortability. The weight becomes expected and the manner in which it delivers its effect is compensated by years of knowing what it can do, and what you can do with it.

Prayer and the prayer warrior are no different in this. A warrior in prayer knows the weight of what they carry and their ability to operate with it. They understand its effect and they know and expect the result it delivers. Ask any prayer warrior who seems to pray and wield prayer with confidence and comfort, and you will find it is because they use it often and have seen it in action. They know their prayer, they know the affect and effect of their prayer, and they have built tremendous confidence in it due to the impact it has in this world. They can see and know what to expect as they have such a deep and real relationship with God that they can read the situation and they know His Word and His Will.

The only people surprised by prayer and who are caught off guard by its use and outcome are those who do not know God or know Him well. I am always amazed when fellow Christians get huge, wide eyes and seem at a loss for words when they see healing occur through prayer and laying on of hands. I always ask them privately if they have a healthy prayer life and if they would like to pray together and be prayer partners. I know they have not really and honestly accepted prayer in their life and they are not using it to the impact and fullness they could be.

This is not a condemnation of them at all, or any kind of holier-than-thou approach...in-fact I always am looking to get my prayer life deeper and more impactful, and these encounters serve me as much as others in seeking God and finding ways to grow my prayer life. If this was a condemnation of anything, it would be the institutions of the church which continue to fail in their mission and their call. The church has either forgotten or just chosen to overlook real, biblical prayer.

When a warrior walks into a room, everyone in the room knows there is a warrior present. You can almost hear the chorus from some 80's action movie song crescendo as you watch them enter any scene or engage in any activity. When a prayer warrior is in the room, everyone should know that a praying man or woman of God is present. The very atmosphere should be charged with the feeling of explosive potential and expectation of the "boom".

Imprecatory Prayer

The Psalms are a powerful place to go when learning about prayer. You will see the depths of the soul as the writer pours out their all into a poetic and at times very heart-wrenching discourse with God. These are the calls upon the supernatural and mighty God of their heart, soul and strength to tear open the veil and to come down into the natural for His people and for His chosen servant.

When it comes to prayer of combat and of battle there is none more pointed and more direct than prayer of imprecation. Imprecatory prayer is prayer which calls down a direct and devastating curse and judgement upon one's enemies. It calls upon the divine to bring swift, and often complete, destruction and immutable decimation to those who are causing harm, great pain, or worse. Imprecatory prayer cuts to the bone with its scathing cry for retribution and justice where and how only God can.

Many today will say that Jesus did away with imprecatory prayer when He said *"Love your enemies, do good to them which hate you, Bless them that curse you, and pray for them which despitefully use you. And unto him that smiteth thee on the one cheek offer also the other"* (Luke 6:27-29). This is not speaking of spiritual warfare and Paul clarifies this, if you will, when he teaches us *"Recompense to no man evil for evil. Provide things honest in the sight of all men. If it be possible, as much as lieth in you, live peaceably with all men. Dearly beloved, avenge not yourselves, but rather give place unto wrath: for it is written, Vengeance is mine; I will repay, saith the Lord."* (Romans 12:17-19)

Paul teaches us, as does Jesus, that we war not against mankind and that it is not our place to seek vengeance and recompense against those who wrong and hurt us. He also teaches us that such justice and action belong to the Lord and to Him alone. This is imprecatory prayer. This is us handing over the course of action against our enemies to the one Almighty, who is ultimately sovereign and whose divine protection rests upon those whom He calls His children.

As we war against darkness and against those overtaken by such nefarious forces it will become necessity to know how to call forth imprecation. To openly and deftly call upon the Lord of hosts to move into action against His foes and upon those who stand to quell all that is light and salt in this world.

Imprecation is verbal, guttural, and comes from ones innermost being to call against the selfish. As it must not be for our gain or carnal delight that we bring these prayers to battle, it must be for God's perfect nature to chase and tear down that which in opposition derides and chides His people. Evil seeks to suppress and oppress God's children and imprecatory prayer breaks the teeth of that prowling lion. Imprecatory prayer calls down the torrent of Holy Spirit fire to catastrophically obliterate Satan's devices and to dismember his hordes and render them inert.

When you read and let the imprecatory prayers in the Psalms go through the filter of your heart you will see the true benefit these bring to our combat. Imprecatory prayer puts the darkness on notice and also can stir the warriors around you to be emboldened and to take heart that God is coming against the fight and night. This is at times why these prayers were used, to encourage and to ignite the fire around them. Imprecatory prayer is a battle cry and a rally cry for Impact Warriors. So, how does one utilize this prayer method and weapon? How do we pray imprecatory prayer?

Application of Imprecation

"The LORD shall cause thine enemies that rise up against thee to be smitten before thy face: they shall come out against thee one way, and flee before thee seven ways." (Deuteronomy 28:7)

To understand the components of imprecation we need to look at Psalms 7, 35, 55, 58, 59, 69, 79, 109, 137 and 139. Here we see several very clear parts to effective impact when we chose to invoke such violence and concentrated power against our spiritual enemies.

First, we see that there is a cry unto the God of our hearts to hear our sufferings and to pay attention to what is occurring against us. We read such lines as *"give ear"* and *"do not hide yourself from my plea"*. Many of the example prayers call upon God to give His notice and attention to the cause and causation of our heartfelt cry.

Second, there is a call to action. There is a fully emotional plea for our Heavenly Father to take up arms for us and to stand up in His assembly. We call unto the Lord Almighty to not sit any longer in this discourse, but to come swiftly between us and our foe. To take action of a most vigorous and violent nature to stop what is occurring and to route those we have come against.

Third, there is a pronouncement against the spiritual powers which are set to be broken and dismayed. This is an indictment against their actions and their move against us. We cannot be shy to proclaim the discourse we have set upon and to clearly state the outcome we know is desired by God in our seeking of His justice and His righteousness. Imprecatory prayer is not a silent and confidential undertaking, it is a loud and emphatic accusation against our adversary.

Fourth, there is a petition for salvation and to be lifted up, above, or away from the issue which triggered this prayer. This is different from the initial heart cry, though sometimes it is part of it. This is not the petition to hear us or notice the situation in which we find ourselves, this is the ask to bring us in close as a part of His intervention. For, like any child, once we know our parent is coming to our rescue all we desire next is for them to hold us and to make us feel that we are secure now. And this is truly the outcome of Spirit-led and Spirit-filled imprecatory prayer.

We see these prayers in the Psalms, they are used by Jesus, and as we have seen they are also taken up by Paul. The main point that is crucial to a working knowledge of imprecation is that we know it is a tool for spiritual warfare. This is not prayer we should ever choose to wield against mankind now that Jesus has called us to think and know this form of prayer differently. We must try to keep our emotions from getting the better of us and from pronouncing anathema too quickly, especially against an individual.

You may ask what the difference is. It is in cursing one who is not really the power behind our pain and suffering.

It is also possible we are cursing without full knowledge of all the details behind what we are facing and what has come upon us.

For this reason, I have always read and seen in imprecatory prayer that the curse and indictment should always be handed over to the Most High. Let God sort out the details and let Him bring down righteous and perfect judgement. Our judgement and righteousness are flawed in that we are stained by sin and within an environment where vision is skewed, and we cannot be disconnected enough from the enemy to be what God is. In my youth and past I have cursed others and prayed imprecatory prayer from a place of the hurt individual who lashed out against the pain. I do not regret what I prayed, but I now understand that what I prayed for was nothing but shallow pleasure sought at the expense of the one who hurt me. Our joy in using imprecatory prayer MUST not come from such sordid pleasure but must come from the joy of seeing the Lord in action toward His people and His purpose. Our joy is in seeing His righteousness and justice brought into this unjust and unrighteous world.

So, with all of this let's look at how and when we would reach into our prayer arsenal and choose this function of prayer. Into the kind of circumstances use of imprecatory prayer is warranted.

Primarily, Imprecatory prayer is a prayer against corporate wrong and injustice. Think of it as a system, a party, or a designated group which has decided to rise up against the Church, against you, or against the truth. In this instance it would be fully agreeable to cast down what they are doing in opposition to God and to call down the intervention of the Almighty. In this instance we have a spiritual rouge power condensed into a larger platform and it is God alone who can destroy their schemes and confuse their plans. It is God alone who can demolish their devices of evil and turn the tide against them sending them fleeing to the hills. In this instance we would find agendas, political motivations, propositions, mob mentalities and tribal inclinations. Praying against those who seek to bring unjust laws into the land and against us, praying against the agendas of Lucifer which we see in some parties, and praying against uprising incited by hysteria. These are examples of what we should bring imprecatory prayer against.

Secondary to the corporate power we see above would be the individual imbued with demonic influence and the powers of darkness behind them. While not traditionally thought of as imprecatory prayer, the pronouncement of Isaiah against the king of Babylon and the same tone used by Ezekiel against the king of Tyre are such a prayer and proclamation. These strongly laid out words are against an individual power and the force(s) behind such. They use the same parts as imprecation found in prayer and they pronounce and bring forth God's justice and judgement. This is how imprecatory prayer can be used against an individual in a biblical way. When we have discerned through the Spirit that what is going on is demonic and at this level of engagement, we must call out the big guns and artillery that was designed for this purpose. Coming against the individual in imprecation while addressing the puppeteer as the root is application of atomic level prayer which removes veils and opens eyes to what is truly at stake and being perpetrated.

Lastly, we would come to application of imprecation against an individual themselves. And as we discussed, I do not see nor understand this to be proper application of Spirit-led and Spirit-filled imprecatory prayer. In all of my studies and experience when it comes to prayer against an individual, if one must engage in this practice, intercession should be sought over imprecation. We will discuss intercession more in this chapter, but for now I want to express that to intercede on one's behalf for their salvation, for their eyes to be opened, and for them to be routed with salvation in mind over judgement is the more appropriate measure. I know that anathemas are given in scripture and also traditionally curses have been levied by Christians many times…but the more I study it I find myself aligned and seeking imprecation in the spiritual always more defensible than against flesh. It is judgment and justice reigned in and rained upon spiritual wickedness; salvation brought as the remedy against flesh.

Prayer of Impartation

"For I long to see you, that I may impart unto you some spiritual gift, to the end ye may be established" (Romans 1:11)

Prayer can be more than just verbal, and prayer of impartation is one such example. In scripture impartation is the gifting or granting to another through spiritual devices. Usually we see this through the laying on of hands in congress with prayer, but it also occurs through prayer alone for God's granting of some spiritual gift to accomplish what has been placed on our heart or shoulders. Think of those times when you pray for wisdom to meet a situation with God's wisdom and not just your own. James tells us quite bluntly that we should pray for wisdom from God if we seek it (James 1:5).

In fact, if you spend enough time in scripture you will see that the impartation most prayed for and sought was always the wisdom of God. But wisdom is but one gift that our Father can impart unto us or grant us in His mercy. We can be imparted with health and life where both have been attacked and being taken from us. We can be gifted with knowledge on something specific that God desires us to know. In fact, almost all of the gifts we see in the prophets are imparted gifts. When Daniel prayed for understanding, it was granted to him. When Daniel prayed to know the king's dream, God allowed him to dream the same dream. When power is imparted to take on the spiritual realm, this is warfare and God granting us all we need for battle.

In the Bible, impartation was an effective and necessary weapon in the spiritual battles we face. This is why the Apostles would ensure the laying on of hands took place when it was called for to impart the gifting of the Holy Spirit so that the emerging 1st century church could have the power to stand in a world of overwhelming darkness spiritually.

Impartation was also seen in the old testament when the patriarchs would pray to impart to the next generation their blessing, or curse. We also see it in the account of Moses when he begins to be overburdened. God tells Moses to call forth seventy elders and that He will take from Moses this burden and grant it unto the seventy (see Numbers 11:16 & 24). The practice of impartation was prevalent in the ancient past and it was alive and practiced as part of the ministry of Jesus Christ and His Church. What the early church knew and utilized as ammunition for combat, we today must understand and bring into our Impact Warfare.

Application of Impartation

Impartation is one of the easier applications of prayer that we can teach on. For some reason this form of prayer is almost self-explanatory and well understood by Christians, but not when it comes to warfare and battle in the supernatural and natural. We use this form of prayer in business when we seek wisdom from God on a deal or to find solutions to complex projects. We use this form of prayer in our personal lives and families when we pray for God to impart healing for a loved one or a friend, when we pray for our own health, wealth, and walk in this life.

When it comes to application of impartation in spiritual warfare, the foremost use is in seeking discernment. Discernment is a particular wisdom, knowledge and understanding of situations, individual motives, and to begin seeing behind the proverbial curtain. Discernment is an integral part of spiritual warfare because without God imparting discernment, we would be blind against our enemies and we would not be able to be effective in ministry (see Philippians 1:9-10). Prayer for discernment in our walk and in our ministry is applied impartation that will profoundly change your life and the way you view the world. It will give you the eyes and heart of God and a peek into the higher dimensions of reality which are more real than what we see and know as real in this world.

When it comes to application of this prayer in your battles and in your life, the only truly necessary thing to comprehend is the strength of God and your weaknesses. Having this fully aware allows you to know what you need and what you lack to be successful and to have impact in the ways God has placed on your heart and to His purpose. Pray for discernment and therefrom you will have the wisdom of God to see what is about you and upon you and you will know at a deep soul level the tools and gifts you will need to survive the fight and have granted by God so that you may continue to stand, to serve, and to have the fullness of impact in this spiritual conflict.

In the use of this method of prayer for battle, it can be thought of as a supply for our needs. We are bringing forward another warrior, whether new to combat or seasoned veteran, and provision is sought that they can have a new gifting which adds to their armament and arsenal. For every warrior, as you grow in your relationship with God and expand in experience, there are new avenues which will be imparted by God to fit the need of where you are serving, and to what you have been asked to do. Many times, we see impartation as the gifting of being a teacher, pastor or prophet and this is true but not the fullness of how gifting works.

With impartation there are only two eternal gifts that God imparts to us. The first is salvation, the second is the indwelling Holy Spirit. Some add righteousness to this, but righteousness is imputed, not imparted...I will save that discussion for another place and time though. Outside of those two, every gift is given for the purposes to which God calls us. This means that the gifts we are given and granted can be for life, for fifteen years, or may be for a short period of ministry we find ourselves thrust into. It is important to note this because if we serve in Christ, we need to apply what we are given and not fake or try to exceed how God desires it be utilized in battle.

"And he gave some, apostles; and some, prophets; and some, evangelists; and some, pastors and teachers; For the perfecting of the saints, for the work of the ministry, for the edifying of the body of Christ" (Ephesians 4:11-12)

If you are imparted the gift of prophecy…then start working as a prophet. But if you find God not working in that gifting but starting to gift you healing, why fight to stay a prophet? Be the healer now that God desires you to be. Application is about knowing and knowing means to have intimate knowledge. This intimate knowledge should be sufficient to guide you in what gift you have and are to operate in at any given time. I know ministers who tell me of how they used to have great success in healing and God worked through them to heal and bring such release and relief, but they no longer see the results. When I ask them to pray and find what gift God now has for them then they scoff at me and say, "God called me to be a healer and that will never change". The truth is only one thing never changes…God. God will gift to you as you need it and in the manner of gifting which will have the greatest impact. Seek this and apply it at His direction and you will see mountains move and the miraculous released.

The last part of this prayer discussion should be on the laying on of hands. This is a ministry function and many times intimately coupled with prayer of impartation. This is a physical, and real touch, from one who is proceeding in prayer to impart, and upon the one to whom the imparted gift is designated and divinely appointed to rest. We must not rush into the laying on of hands or to approaching this exchange without discernment. This is clearly spelled out in the interaction between Peter and Simon Magus in Acts 8:9-24. To this day the act of trying to pay for impartation and position is known as simony and is detestable.

Impartation is never for sale, and it is never guaranteed to anyone. We do not earn anything imparted unto us by God through prayer or the laying on of hands... it is granted and gifted, not earned!

This is a lesson I have seen people struggle with internally as well as in the prayer and working of impartation. We are never owed anything in this life, this is a lesson to know and understand as it will give you perspective and gratitude. Years of ministry does not mean you deserve to be imparted with anything. Being placed in a position by man does not entitle you to anything. Advanced degrees, how much you give or donate, who you know, and what you want matter little in this exchange. God's gifts are His alone to grant and His servants who pray and lay hands in His Spirit will only do so as He directs. Never compromise or be swayed by the reasoning of mankind or the spiritual. Impart and pray for impartation to God's desire and let anyone who feels slighted take that up with God. Be true to Him always.

Intercessory Prayer

"O Lord, according to all thy righteousness, I beseech thee, let thine anger and thy fury be turned away from thy city Jerusalem, thy holy mountain: because for our sins, and for the iniquities of our fathers, Jerusalem and thy people are become a reproach to all that are about us. Now therefore, O our God, hear the prayer of thy servant, and his supplications, and cause thy face to shine upon thy sanctuary that is desolate, for the Lord's sake. O my God, incline thine ear, and hear; open thine eyes, and behold our desolations, and the city which is called by thy name: for we do not present our supplications before thee for our righteousnesses, but for thy great mercies. O Lord, hear; O Lord, forgive; O Lord, hearken and do; defer not, for thine own sake, O my God: for thy city and thy people are called by thy name." (Daniel 9:16-19)

Daniel chapter nine is an introductory lesson in proper intercessory prayer. Daniel is grieved and calls unto his Father in heaven to hear and come intervene in the course of what His children Israel are captive to. Daniel interceded on behalf of his people and brought before the Lord the supplications and cries of those who themselves were not seeking with such fervency their deliverance according to His promise. This is Daniel engaged in Impact Warfare. How do we know this was active spiritual warfare? Because the angel Gabriel himself recounts to Daniel the battle raging and caused by his petition and prayer to God.

When most people think of spiritual warfare prayer, they mention intercessory prayer. This is because some of the most impactful prayer warriors we read of were masters of intercessory prayer. Men and women who give of themselves fully to the cause and to the case of others in such a way that they are filled with the desire to see God work where others do not call for him, and where others may not be able to. When we speak of the writer of all prayer and to whom we must look as the mentor par excellence on prayer we see He is the ultimate intercessor, and this is the chief part of His battle in the supernatural on our behalf. Jesus Christ is our intercessor, in complete congress with the Holy Spirit, He intercedes and shows us the importance of intercessory prayer in our walk and in our imitation of Him in ministry (see Romans 8:34).

Application of intercessory prayer

There is no further need to elucidate what intercessory prayer is. Jesus gives us the prime definition and example, and apart from Daniel we see this form of prayer taken up by almost every prayer warrior in scripture. It is quite obviously the act of praying on behalf of another for direct impact and fervent intervention by God.

But how are we to intercede? We are to intercede by the guiding of the Holy Spirit (Romans 8:26-27). We are to intercede as a necessary function of our being as we could never do less as it would hurt our heart and be found as sin to our soul (1 Samuel 12:23). Intercession is close in relation to imprecatory prayer in how it should be wielded and effectively used in our prayer arsenal.

You may be asking, how is it anything like imprecatory prayer? Well, it is exactly like imprecatory prayer in that it has all four parts that we discussed and has the same charge when utilized, but where imprecation is a curse called down upon another…intercession is a call to fight for another. Intercessory prayer is to bring blessings, to bring healing, to bring deliverance, and to fight on behalf of another where imprecation is to curse and ask God to fight against another.

Intercessory prayer is powerful, as it sets self aside and is a side to prayer which thwarts Satan's attacks and his hold on those he otherwise would conquer easily… they have been tricked into believing their voice cannot be heard or of any use, and so we lift ours. Intercessory prayer also has its power in agreement. When we pray and intercede for another and it joins with their prayers and the Will of God, we have agreement with power like no other to shake the heavens and to bring change and breakthrough where all seemed hopeless.

I would like to introduce you to someone who every prayer warrior should know. There is a powerful book written by Norman Grubbs called *"Rees Howells: Intercessor"*. It is a book about a man who embraced intercessory prayer like no one today does and this is not a man from ancient times or a bygone era of mystics and saints. Rees Howells was a twentieth century man who knew the power of relying on God for everything and when he brought his knees and prayer into intercession…the spiritual realm shook and the supernatural became alive and real in this world.

When it came to super-charging my intercessory prayer it was scripture and this book which opened my eyes and really brought me to a place where prayer becomes impactful and where I saw spiritual warfare become the most effective in my ministry it has ever been.

151

If I had to say what the most important factor to intercessory prayer is, and to its effective application in combat... it would be heart. To really epitomize spiritual warfare intercessory prayer, you must have a burning in your heart for the situation and for others who are fighting in this war alongside us. If you are just going through the steps to place someone in prayer...you are not an intercessor. If you pray for intercession because others seem to really care about the issue, and you care about them...you are not an intercessor. If you cannot sleep without placing someone in prayer because the thought of one more moment of them not having salvation or supply to their need weighs heavily upon your heart and the only release is to release it to the Father and to press against the forces which wish to squash your intercessory prayer...then you are an intercessor. If the cause you bring before God causes you to tear up and to be unhinged from your comfort until you can bring the Almighty into the conversation...then you are an intercessor.

Intercessory prayer in spiritual battle is a long-term pursuit. When you read of great intercessors you see one common thread and that is fervent and continual prayer, even if it takes years. When someone or something has such weight in your heart there will never be a time on your knees when you do not bring it before God. It becomes a constant discussion between you and the Lord as you continually let Him know the condition of your heart.

As we saw with Daniel, many times any delay we see in our intercessory prayer being fulfilled and answered is not on the part of God. The moment Daniel thought to bring his prayer before the Lord an answer was dispatched. It was warfare and the battle in the spiritual realm which hindered its delivery. So, never think to stop because God does not care as you do, or even imagine He does not feel the weight of your heart and need. Press on as He will continue to hear and to answer from His heart. What we need to have is patience and to wait on the Lord for His timing and to listen and watch for His reply and response. Sometimes it may be different from what we desire, but it will be His desire. Sometimes it will be delayed, but it was never delayed for lack of care or urgency.

The story of Daniel at the Hiddekel river brings me to one last thing I would like to interject into our discussion on prayer in spiritual warfare. That is for us to never lose sight of what warfare is and that it is not being fought in the highest heavens. The warfare we are engaged with is taking place in the natural but only as a result of the supernatural realm spilling into our dimension of reality. Just like any battle and war we see in this realm, the battles of the spiritual realm have two sides, and each is fighting with intensity, power, and its own warriors called to impact.

This means that the other side of this conflict will work against your prayer and against your impact ministry every day and every moment where they are allowed. We know this exists now and we have been shown its reality in scripture. With this we then know that with all of the prayer and battle we stand in we must pray against these forces of evil and darkness. This is why Paul tells us who our real opponents are, because he knew we had to come against them if we are to serve and work in the power and Spirit of God.

When you pray, whether imprecatory, impartation, or intercessory, do so with the strength of conviction we have discussed but also with the follow-through that we now see must be there. Pray against their schemes and tactics. Pray against the delay and their entrapment of our answers and interaction with God.

The full forces of the "ruler of this world" will make use of distraction, depression, stress, and inconvenience to pull you away from everything we have discussed in this book. They will be successful at times, because they are very skilled at what they do and how they do it. But they are never more skilled than God and cannot succeed where we have brought him to the fight. Remember this, use this in your prayer. Tip each spear with the additional prayer of breakthrough and to not be hindered by the weakness of wickedness that will knowingly come against it and you.

Impact Warrior Prayer in Impact Warfare

This part of the book was an insight into the life of an Impact Warrior. An Impact Warrior is a prayer warrior. Their life, their mission, their ministry, their breath, their joy, their all is wrapped in some way, shape, or form in prayer.

Impact Warrior Prayer is prayer without ceasing in that every moment and breath is a form and function of prayer. There is no part or portion of life which is kept from God, not that one could keep anything from God, as they seek and relish in the sharing of every second with the divine. This is also true of warfare and how there is no move or action entered into without prayer guiding, prayer moving, and prayer impacting the battlefield around us. Prayer is absolute atomic, ground-quaking, heaven-shaking raw power from the person of God.

In Ephesians we were shown the Armor of God. While each and every part of that armor can be a weapon when worn and wielded by an Impact Warrior, we are expressly given two very powerful weapons which go hand-in-hand. We have for battle the Sword of the Spirit and Prayer. We have the Word of God and our words in God. Both the sword and our prayer MUST be Spirit-filled, and the Holy Spirit must season and empower each.

It is the Word of God which is our primary instructor, through the Spirit, in prayer. It is the Word of God that we have in scripture which gives us the Will and character of God manifest before us so that we may know Him, and we may grow in our relationship with Him. This spiritual growth and relationship are dependent on prayer. Scripture becomes the sword which we brandish with confidence as we become one with God and know His Word so much so that they become our own words as we navigate and engage with the spiritual and natural worlds. That knowledge and wisdom of God in His Word then flavors and sharpens our prayer so that it becomes the spear by which we penetrate the strongholds before us, and we launch our aerial attacks against the pressing darkness and the powers and rulers of wickedness.

Impact Warrior Prayer is something like a weapon of mass destruction against the forces of evil in this world. Just as a nuclear explosion blasts through the thick clouds to clear the skies of all but its force and destruction. So, our prayer clears the atmosphere of darkness as the presence of God illuminates the air with its detonation of appearance into the conflict. Our prayer leaves no strongholds standing, no battlements secure, and no chains left tethered as all is swept away in the power of God's active movement into the fight for His children and His divine purpose. In His presence no sin can stand, and no rebellion can have power any longer. There is no fight against the Holy Spirit, and against God's people who are filled and sealed with Him.

Imagine the scene when Elijah brought down fire from heaven to consume everything on the altar in the presence of the priests of Ba'al and Israel. This was an all-consuming eruption of unequaled and unparalleled magnitude and it left no question as to who had just moved and who was the Living God (see 1 Kings 18:20-40). This is what an Impact Warrior delivers when they bring forth Impact Prayer. The force of what they bring to bear in the Spirit is like a mighty pillar of all-consuming fire which leaves nothing behind and nothing undeclared. The effective and fervent prayer of a prayer warrior lets everyone know who God is and that He is real! They never leave the impression that they have done anything or that they are anything...the only impression left behind is the very impression of the hand of God who has come down and who has delivered His message.

We are to seek prayer such as this. We must step away from prayer which is rote or routine. Even if we routinely go into prayer...there is nothing routine or mundane about how we become enraptured and filled with His Holy Spirit and the fullness of His Presence. If you are not feeling and living in this kind of active and powerful prayer, then go into the prayer you know and ask God to be real before you and to become real in your life and in your battles. Take even one step further into the deep, and God will close the distance and bring you to this place of Impact Prayer.

IMPACT WARFARE

Conclusion: Impact Warfare

"But we are not of them who draw back unto
perdition; but of them that believe to the saving of the soul."
(Hebrews 10:39)

This work was put together to stir your innermost being to action. To find within you the spark that is there and ready to become a blazing firestorm of impact in the world. Spiritual warfare is very real, and if you have not heard this before then you have now…it is more real than the reality we know and live within.

Evil is real and there are entities which embrace this darkness and embody the titles of principalities, powers, rulers, etc. Today we too quickly dismiss the supernatural and underestimate the power that is at play around us. Every facet of our life is exposed to these forces and in many ways controlled by them for some, if not all, of our lives. What has changed the rulership and authority under which you now live is that you have accepted Jesus Christ into your heart, been filled with the Holy Spirit, and embraced in the arms of your almighty Father.

We began by speaking a lot about the makeup of an Impact Warrior. The introduction of illustration into how warfare is alike between the natural and supernatural was important to paint the picture of how serious and intense battle is and why it is so important to understand our place in it. Your place is as an adopted son or daughter of God. You are adopted into a family of warriors without equal, and they have called you into the service of their warfare with all you need in Him to be an impact of such magnitude and power that no fight is even close to fair.

This is why my heart aches to hear Christians speak of defeat and struggle in their spiritual warfare. This is why I have developed and begun to separate spiritual warfare in general from what I call Impact Warfare.

Spiritual warfare is something we all engage in, live in, and find ourselves surrounded by. Spiritual warfare is in everything and every interaction we have in this world. Every single person alive is in spiritual warfare. What differentiates Christians is that they know this and are called to engage it. This does not mean we always know how to engage or even that we catch on quickly enough that a battle is being waged as we have discussions, interact with others, or simply just be pouring our morning coffee. But we are in battle and it is when we recognize this and step into it armored, armed and standing in the Holy Spirit that we have marched into this spiritual warfare prepared and set for Impact Warfare.

Impact Warfare is the raw and unrestricted power of God flowing into battle through His children. It is the direct objection to all of the wickedness and nonsense of this age and day. We stand in battle that prophets spoke of and which all of time has been marching towards. For centuries and millennia groans have been getting greater and the pangs of birth into this end-times fray become stronger. The crescendo of God's plan and purpose is reaching its climax. With it, we are seeing the last dying rage of Lucifer as he gathers the powers of darkness and despair to come against God's chosen people and His Church.

This is not a simple fight. This is not a light skirmish. This is full scale dimensional terror being unleashed in the bloodiest conflict creation has ever witnessed. This depth of combat is not for the arrogant or ignorant to win but has been given to the humble and wise in Christ. God moves with the banner of His victory before Him, and He calls you to march under that banner in any, and all, of your struggles and battles.

This book is a shot to the soul and a clarion cry to the Church and to you. Rise up and return to His arms. Turn from this world and toward the God of Heaven so that He may richly and abundantly set you up for warfare. Return to the front lines of this battle bearing the Armor of God and wielding the Sword of the Spirit and Impact Prayer! Come to the front with all of the power of God and do not shirk, do not be squeamish, and do not for one second give up one ounce of territory. We are called through impact to take back territory, to route the schemes of evil, and to bring the Gospel message to our day and to every ear that can hear.

You are the impact of God's plan and His desire. You are a warrior without compare and when you stride in the fire of the Holy Spirit the atmosphere around you and the air you breath becomes so charged and radiated with the power of God that prayer takes on the place for which it was designed and the supernatural is driven to its knees proclaiming the sovereign God and Jesus Christ as Lord.

Take to heart all we have discussed. Know that this book is not a comprehensive compendium, as I have stated before, but is here to remind you and refresh you in truth and in the language of warfare in the spiritual. This book is to tell you to stop lying where you have come against the battle and have been wounded and beaten. Stand to your feet and be resupplied with the Holy Spirit and move in the impact prayer of a combat general. You are the pinnacle of all weapons against Satan and the fallen angels. Never forget for a single heartbeat that what courses through you is God and who you serve is God and your savior and salvation is God!

Every single breath is an invitation to take stock and to re-center and focus your walk in Jesus. So, take a big breath in, set your eyes and heart on Jesus, and let's get ready to rejoin the battle, engaging end-times spiritual warfare in dynamic prayer and with maximum impact.

Bibliography

This entire book rests on the Holy Bible as its guide, influence, and is the source of all material. I have used the King James Version of the Bible, but I encourage everyone reading to find a good translation and begin reading it today!

To grow in your relationship with Jesus Christ, please read the gospels of Matthew, Mark, Luke and John; all found in "The New Testament". Listen to the Gospel message and accept Jesus Christ as your Lord and Savior. Time is running out and today is the day to come home; your Father is waiting for you!

Other Sources Used:
Grubb, Norman. *Rees Howells: Intercessor.* CLC Publications, 1952.
Merriam-Webster's Dictionary (online resource 12/2019)
Dictionary.com (online resource 12/2019)
Wikipedia.com (online resource 12/2019)

IMPACT WARFARE

About the Author

B. James Howells is known for his intense, no-nonsense, speaking and teaching style; and he is frequently sought after for his expertise on spiritual warfare, deliverance, prophecy, the occult and supernatural. With thirty years of biblical research and study, along with over fifteen years in ministry, James has an approach that shows experience in many walks of life and a unique understanding of perspective.

James is the Founder & Director of Watchfire Ministries; a spiritual warfare, apologetics and prophecy ministry based out of Tampa / St. Pete, Florida; he is the host of "The Watchfire Report"; and he hosts and/or has taken part in numerous conferences, workshops, podcasts, multi-media projects, and video ministry.

To learn more about B. James Howells, to see his teachings, read more about what he does, and to check out upcoming events and schedule please visit www.watchfire.tv

IMPACT WARFARE

IMPACT WARFARE

IMPACT WARFARE

IMPACT WARFARE

IMPACT WARFARE

Printed in Great Britain
by Amazon

13152960R00099